brides bible

everything you need to know to plan the perfect wedding

Contents

Text by Sara Burford.
This edition published in 2009 by L&K Designs.
© L&K Designs 2009
PRINTED IN CHINA

Publishers Disclaimer

Whilst every effort has been made to ensure that the information contained is correct, the publisher cannot be held responsible for any errors and or omissions.

Firstly, congratulations on your engagement! You're about to dive headfirst into one of the most incredible and exciting journeys of your life, starting with the process of planning your wedding, through to becoming a newly wedded couple. If it all feels a little overwhelming, that's completely natural, it might only be one day you're planning for, but it takes months of planning to get there. There's a lot to think about and do… which is where the Bride's Bible comes in!

You might already know what you want for your wedding, or you may have no clue at all… but whatever your starting point, this comprehensive guide will help you with all the major aspects of preparing for your wedding including tradition and etiquette, bridal wear and wedding suppliers, a must-have guide to bridal health and beauty, great money-saving tips and much, much more.

Set out in easy-to-read sections, this book provides any bride-to-be with a wealth of useful facts and information, essential timetables and checklists and even some useful insights into the first tentative steps of marriage.

Written in an accessible and light-hearted style, the Bride's Bible will become a valuable resource to you through this wonderfully exciting and joyful time.

BUT before you start planning and organising anything; make absolutely sure that you revel in your engagement - be that a party, a special dinner, shouting it from the rooftops or just kissing each other a million times over and nauseating everyone around you!

Whatever you do, enjoy it – this is such a precious time and you'll want to remember these feelings forever, so don't rush them.

Planning & Scheduling

Starting Out... Planning Tips & Advice

When faced with the task of organising a wedding, it can be a daunting experience – how on earth can you almost single-handedly take on such a gargantuan task? And how can you avoid turning into your own personal version of 'Bridezilla' during moments of wedding oriented stress and strain? You want to look and feel like a princess, not act like a spoilt, grumpy one! The simple answer is 'planning'. The more you plan, the more successful you'll be. Of course, best laid plans... often go awry... but essentially, if you approach your wedding as a project to be managed, you'll have a much better chance of achieving the results you want and minimising your stress levels. Ergo, you're far less likely to turn into Medusa's less-nice sister! Here are a few handy pointers to help you begin...

Checklists
Keep yourself focused and organised by using a checklist. You'll find a great wedding schedule and task list later in this section; detailing all the integral steps of planning a successful wedding.

Get Help!
Rather than plan every last detail by yourselves; why not ask for a little help along the way? Whether you choose the professional help of a wedding consultant/coordinator, or the help of trusted friends and family who have experience of planning their own weddings; it can be really beneficial to get other people's input, help and ideas.

Guest Lists
Once you've thrashed out your guest list, make sure that you keep an up-to-date list, just in case any last minute changes are made. Ideally, your list will have contact addresses and phone numbers. A computerised version is probably the least time consuming and easy to update – just don't forget to back it up!

Research
Before making any radical decisions for your wedding, make sure that you do your research! Draw on every resource you can think of; magazines, wedding TV channels, the internet, books, brochures, wedding supplier outlets, friends and family... even films!

Research Organiser

Make an ideas-board, organiser or scrapbook; this way you can keep all your cuttings, printings, swatches, ideas and inspirations for your wedding in one easily accessible place, (keeping the dress under close-wraps of course!). It will help you and your fiancé in the decision making processes.

Wedding Consultants/Coordinators

The concept of professional wedding help is one that will probably divide the population into those who think that it's the best, and only, way to plan a wedding; and those who think it's a step too far into indulgence and who would recoil at being 'told' what would work best for their special day.

But, whatever your leaning, the reality is that if you and your partner are busy professionals, time-pushed parents, or even just feeling a little overwhelmed and lost in having to put together your wedding day – a wedding professional may be an invaluable asset in helping you to realise your wedding day dreams and assisting you with all the intricacies involved in organising a successful day.

Wedding professionals will guide you through the process of decision making and organisation; getting to know you and your fiancé, taking into account your likes and dislikes and working with the theme and feel that you want to give to your wedding. Fielding any problems and allaying any wedding day fears, they can act as an important touch-stone at a time when you will need to feel that someone really knows what they're doing.

They will also use their knowledge, contacts and expertise in booking your suppliers; cake, flowers, transport, venue, etc... saving you invaluable time, effort and money. And as for last minute snags, not a problem!

If you decide to use a wedding professional, make sure that you do your research. Look up reviews and ask for references; meet each one in person before you make a decision and let them sell themselves to you; have your questions ready and if you feel uneasy with someone, they're absolutely not for you. You will also find that some venues have a wedding co-ordinator available to you so check before booking any additional services.

Wedding Forums

The internet has a plethora of sites and forums dedicated to all-things-bridal; ranging from the thrilling stages of your initial engagement through to living life after the big day itself. You can chat to other engaged couples, get sound advice from people who have already walked down the aisle, pick up great supplier tips and get valuable help in planning your dream honeymoon.

First-Steps Planning Questionnaire

Before you start doing your research and making decisions, first stop and take stock of what you and your fiancé envisage for your special day. It's no good you thinking, "Pink, glitter, tiaras, golden thrones, horse-drawn chariots...", if he's thinking, "Suave, sophisticated, James-Bond-esque, roulette, dancing girls..." You get the picture! You both have the right to independent views and tastes, but it's essential to make sure that you start off on the same page. To avoid arguments and misunderstandings, (a.k.a. 'stuff him, I'm going to book what I want anyway'), further down the line; take time to do this simple, but informative, questionnaire. Not only will it help you to avoid non-refundable impulsive decision making, it will also help you give suppliers the answers to standard questions that they will ask. Whether you choose to fill this out as a couple, or independently, this as a good starting point for initial discussions and ideas.

Circle which words best describe how you want your wedding to be.

Modern	Old-Fashioned	Formal	Relaxed
Classy	Tasteful	Fun	Different
Religious	Secular	Romantic	Classic
Casual	Themed	Traditional	Glamorous
Funky	Well coordinated	Bright	Loving
Unique	Elegant	Luxurious	Decadent
Expensive	Memorable	Cute	Kitsch
Warm	Welcoming	Minimalist	Trendy
Theatrical	Morning	Afternoon	Evening
Children	Adults-Only	Outdoors	Entertaining
Marquee	'Wow'-Factor	Intimate	Personal

Choose your preferences from the following; I want to get married...

On our engagement/first date anniversary ☐

On Valentines Day/Christmas Eve/New Year's Eve, etc ☐

On another 'special' date ☐

In 1-2 years ☐

In 2-4 years ☐

In spring ☐

In summer ☐

In autumn ☐

In winter ☐

In another country ☐

Although you won't have come up with a definitive budget yet, choose a price range within which you would like your wedding costs to come.

Less than	£2,500	☐
Between	£2,500 - £5,000	☐
Between	£5,000 - £10,000	☐
Between	£10,000 - £20,000	☐
Between	£30,000 – £40,000	☐
Between	£40,000 - £50,000	☐
More than	£50,000	☐

Rate [in order of importance] **how you most want to remember your wedding day.**

How romantic it was ☐

How happy our parents were ☐

How happy our guests were ☐

How happy and in love we both were ☐

How traditional and 'proper' it was ☐

How exciting and fun it was ☐

How beautiful and elegant it was ☐

How modern and classy it was ☐

How unique it was ☐

How smoothly and seamlessly everything went ☐

Rate [in order of importance] **what is most important to you on the day.**

Enjoyment of family & friends ☐

Clothing & accessories (bride, groom, attendants) ☐

Wedding rings ☐

Venue aesthetics (flowers, decoration, centrepieces, lighting, etc) ☐

Atmosphere & ambience ☐

Spirituality ☐

Musical entertainment (DJ, live band, solo singer, karaoke, etc) ☐

Other entertainment (games, performers, fireworks, etc) ☐

Quality food ☐

Alcohol ☐

Novelty or unusual feature (ice sculpture, chocolate fountain, etc) ☐

Photographer ☐

Videographer ☐

The order in which you've rated each choice will help you to decide how your budget is best divided.

Choose a few colour options for your wedding day and write them down as discussion points.

1)

2)

3)

4)

5)

Any other "must have" or considerations

Your Essential Wedding Planner

This is a wonderfully exhilarating and magical time for you and there will be a million and one things running through your head; what will you wear? Where will you get married? What will your colour scheme be? Where will your honeymoon be? Who will you invite… the list will seem endless. In these initial stages it will be easy to go off on a tangent and to start focusing on things that, although exciting, aren't priority in terms of your long term wedding plans. So to keep yourself on track and organised, start your wedding planning process with this user-friendly planner and check list; taking you through all your plans in easy time-scheduled sections.

To Do As Soon As Possible

 Tell your relatives and closest friends of your exciting news, (if you haven't already!)

 Decide on the type of ceremony you and your fiancé would like, i.e. religious or civil.

 Set a provisional date for your wedding.

 If you opt for a religious ceremony, arrange a meeting with your priest, minister or rabbi.

 If you choose a civil ceremony, book the registry office or civil ceremony venue – remember that if you choose a civil ceremony venue, rather than a registry office, you will need to check that a registrar is available to come out to your venue on your date.

 Check the requirements regarding marriage certificates and other associated legal requirements; e.g. notice to the Superintendant Registrar for civil ceremonies and publication of the banns for a religious ceremony.

 Set a realistic budget and decide, between yourselves and both sets of parents, who will be paying for what.

Choose your chief bridesmaid, best man and other attendants; remembering to make sure they're available and willing.

 Compile a provisional guest list and see where that brings you to in terms of guest numbers – it may help to run your list past both sets of parents, to make sure that you've remembered all relevant family members.

 Discuss your options for ceremony and reception venues and make appointments to see them – if your choice is a popular venue, don't delay in booking it!

 At least make a provisional booking for your favourite venues and give yourself a little thinking time to make your decision. Go back and visit your shortlist choices if you're struggling to decide between them.

 Once you've chosen your venue, decide on your timings – discuss these with the venue, just to make sure that they can accommodate your ideas.

 Once you're happy with your timing, confirm any provisional bookings for your ceremony and reception.

 Decide on your wedding colours with your fiancé. Sometimes it's a nice idea to theme the colour on his preferred choice of waistcoat, rather than the other way around! Remember that you're likely to make a lot of decisions about how the wedding looks – and importantly, you get to wear the dress of your dreams, not what anyone else has chosen for you – so this is an opportunity for him to feel that what he would like to wear is as important.

 If you want to hire a wedding planner or professional consultant, then it's better to do it sooner rather than later – especially if your wedding is during peak season.

 Send out 'save-the-date' cards, if you're planning to.

8 to 10 Months Before

 Shop for your wedding dress – remember that you'll need plenty of time for a made-to-measure dress to be ordered.

 Once you've chosen your dress, shop for shoes and accessories. Start shopping for your attendants dresses.

 Book your photographer, (and videographer, if you're using one – check with your venue/officiant about their rules around videoing the ceremony).

 Organise wedding insurance.

 Provisionally book the bridal suite for your wedding night.

 Discuss menu options with an external caterer, (if you're having one), and arrange a tasting appointment.

 Discuss menu options and drinks packages with in-house reception venue caterers. Arrange a tasting appointment.

 Book your DJ and/or live entertainment for the evening.

 Order your wedding cake – make sure you taste samples!

 Start thinking about your honeymoon destination.

 Discuss your wedding flower ideas with a florist.

 Book your transport to and from your ceremony and reception venues – remembering attendants and parents too.

Notes

6 to 8 Months Before

 Begin your personal beauty and health routine. Get some advice if you feel you would benefit from a professional opinion.

 Confirm your menu and drink choices with your caterer.

 If you are a having a religious ceremony, discuss readings and music with your Priest, Minister or Rabbi – book your ceremony musicians.

 If you're having a civil ceremony, discuss any readings and music you would like to include and have them agreed by your officiant.

 Order your invitations, menus and place cards.

 Decide on your flower choices and book your florist.

 Book your honeymoon and any transport needed to take you to your first-night hotel, or the airport. Confirm your bridal suite booking.

 Find out if you need any visas, inoculations or courses of medication, (e.g. malaria tablets), for your honeymoon destination.

Notes

4 to 6 Months Before

 Book a consultation with your hairdresser and discuss possible styles. Don't forget to book them for the day!

 Remind your fiancé to get his and his attendant's outfits.

 Choose gifts for the best man, attendants, mothers and any helpers.

 Confirm your order of service and have it printed.

 If you are changing your name, renew your passport. Your officiating religious representative or registrar will need to sign your form for you. Remind your fiancé to check that his passport is valid for your honeymoon date.

 Compile a gift list and register it with your chosen retail company.

 Choose and order wedding favours.

 Start to plan your rehearsal dinner and tot up numbers of guests.

 Reserve any rental equipment you might need, e.g. dishes, tables, chairs, tents, porta-loos, linen, etc.

 Book a calligrapher to write your invitations, place cards, etc – if you're having one.

 Choose your wedding rings.

 Start experimenting with make-up, or visit a beautician and have a trial make-up session.

 Discuss your hen-night celebrations with your attendants – time to let your hair down!

 Shop til you drop! Treat yourself to some new clothes for your honeymoon – and don't forget your 'going-away' outfit!

2 to 4 Months Before

 Send out invitations, venue/accommodation details and directions, menu choices, gift lists and any other information for your guests. This can be done altogether – or you can choose to send out an information pack, once guests have confirmed their attendance.

 Keep an updated list of acceptances and refusals.

 Make sure that any accommodation has been booked for family members.

 For your religious ceremony, book your rehearsal time and date.

 Check with your fiancé that he and his attendants are on track for the day and that their outfits have been ordered.

 Book beauty treatments, such as; fake tan, nails, waxing, etc.

 Purchase any new make-up needed for your wedding day 'look'.

 If you're choosing to make a speech, start preparing your ideas.

 Discuss special requests and playlist choices with your DJ or band; including your first dance.

 Write or choose your wedding vows.

Notes

1 to 2 Months Before

 Confirm final guest numbers and other details with your reception venue and/or caterers. Contact any guests that you have not received an RSVP from.

 Have your final trial with your hairdresser before the 'big-day'!

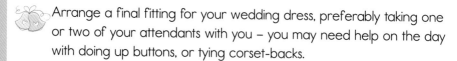 Arrange a final fitting for your wedding dress, preferably taking one or two of your attendants with you – you may need help on the day with doing up buttons, or tying corset-backs.

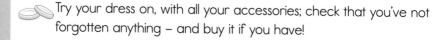 Try your dress on, with all your accessories; check that you've not forgotten anything – and buy it if you have!

 Draw up a seating plan for your guests.

 Finalise your speech details and practice it.

 Re-confirm bookings with suppliers and deliveries to the venue; e.g. cake, flowers. Arrange delivery of button holes and corsages for the day.

 Order your honeymoon currency.

 Make a list of must-have photo shots and agree it with your photographer.

 If you're changing your surname, write to banks, doctors, Inland Revenue and any other official bodies you need to.

 Wear in your wedding shoes a little, by wearing them around the house.

2 Weeks Before

 Have your final haircut and colour before the wedding.

 Attend your rehearsal dinner, if you're having one.

 Time for your respective hen and stag parties! Enjoy!

1 Week Before

 Rehearsal at the church or venue, if applicable.

 Start to pack for your honeymoon.

 Collect honeymoon currency.

 Check tickets, passports, transport and any other travel requirements.

 Go through any last minute details with your attendants, venue and suppliers.

 Send out 'thank you' notes to any guests who have sent gifts.

The Day Before

 Attend your beauty treatment appointments; nails, fake tan, etc.

 Arrange for your luggage and any other necessary items to go to your reception venue.

 Help to decorate your reception area, if necessary.

 Invite your closest friends over, or go out for a meal with them – relax and enjoy their company; it'll help with your nerves. But don't stay out too late or drink too much! Go home and have a nice, relaxing bath. Make yourself a milky drink and go to bed early.

On The Big Day!

 Get up early, so that you give yourself plenty of time to relax and get ready. The last thing you want is to be rushing.

 Make sure that you eat breakfast; your nerves may tell you you're not hungry, but you'll feel and operate better if you have something in your stomach.

 Have your hair and make-up done.

 Get dressed, with the help of your chosen attendant(s).

 The mother-of-the-bride and bridesmaids leave for the ceremony first; followed by the bride and her father.

 Time to make an entrance and enjoy your day!

The Perfect Day

The Perfect Day

With so much to organise, plan and pay for – you'll no doubt be opting for professional assistance with things such as flowers, wedding cake, transport, catering, photography, stationery, etc. This section will help by pointing you in the right direction, providing you with useful tips and ways to avoid the pitfalls of finding the ideal supplier.

First, some general tips to remember:-
Once you've set your budget, do your utmost to stick to it. If you start juggling supplier costs, you're at risk of spending more than you anticipated.

In the interests of practicality and peace of mind, it's best to source suppliers which are local to your venue. Recommendations are great, but if your wedding cake supplier is 50 miles away, you're opening yourself up to potential problems on the day.

Meet all your suppliers in person, so that you can get a feel for their general demeanour. These people will play a pivotal role in the organisation of your wedding, so it's important that you can form a good rapport with them.

Make sure that you really know what you're buying and ask to see/taste samples of each supplier's work. A good supplier will expect you to ask.

Be very specific in terms of agreeing a contract, down to brand names, exact flower choices, timing, etc.

Ask all of your suppliers for a detailed quote. You don't want any nasty surprises in the shape of hidden charges.

Be prepared to pay deposits for all your suppliers which can be anything from 10% to 50%.

Contact your suppliers a couple of weeks before the wedding just to reconfirm details and agree any last minute tweaks.

Cakes

Your wedding cake is a small, but classically significant part of your day. As the traditional symbol of the beginning of sharing the rest of your lives together, the cutting of the cake is a much anticipated part of your wedding ceremony – so picking the right cake for you is going to be an important part of your preparations.

Be Creative

Use as many different sources as you can for inspiration for your cake. Take pictures to suppliers if you've found something you like – or make a sketch, if you've a specific idea in your head.

Be creative and use shapes, motifs, fabrics or decorations from your wedding to use when designing your wedding cake such as flowers from your bouquet, fabric matching your dress or decorations which match your theme. A good wedding cake supplier should be able to advise you on the best choices, both aesthetically and practically.

Booking

Give yourself 8-10 months before your wedding to source and order your wedding cake. Good wedding cake suppliers will get very busy in peak seasons, so be sure to book your favourite early enough.

Budget Savvy

If you've found the perfect design for a cake, but having it made for 120+ guests is going to have some unsavoury ramifications on your budget, ask your cake-maker to downsize the size of the cake and to supply a 'kitchen cake'. This comes as a standard sheet cake, with the same coloured icing – your guests will never know the difference!

Cake Stand & Knife

Ask whether your cake supplier will provide a cake stand and knife, if not, make sure that your wedding breakfast venue has a good, solid cake stand and cake knife. It's one of the smaller details that you don't want to forget.

Compare Suppliers

Meet at least 3 wedding cake suppliers that way you'll have 3 sets of prices, designs and personalities to compare. You'll need to consider all factors when making a decision.

Coordination

When choosing your cake, think about the overall theme, colours and mood of your wedding day. It'll be the centre of attention when it comes to cutting it, so you'll want it to do you proud.

Delivery

If possible, opt for your cake to be delivered by your supplier – it's one less stress for you to have to worry about on your wedding day. Just ensure that the delivery charge is included in your final quote.

Different Flavours

Although traditional, not everyone likes fruit cake, so consider other fillings for each cake tier. Your cake designer should be able to advise you on popular choices and how best to layer the cake.

Formal or Informal

For a very traditional and formal wedding, a white or cream cake is often best suited to the occasion. Coloured, novelty or cupcakes are often best suited to more informal affairs.

Tasting Sessions!

When sourcing your wedding cake supplier, make sure you have fun tasting their wares! And take some home for your fiancé if he's not with you... if it makes the car journey home!

Catering

Alcohol

Do your caterers supply the alcohol? Or would it be cheaper to buy your own alcohol and pay corkage at the venue? Check out the possibilities with prospective caterers. If you order cases of alcohol from an online source, your purchases can be delivered direct to your venue. If you feel this is a smart option for you, make sure that you check the corkage charges at your choice of venue first.

Check Out Premises

It's a good idea to call in and see your caterers at their premises. That way you can better gauge what kind of operation they run and discuss things with them at a more detailed level. Request a check of their kitchen facilities, including their crockery, table linen and plates as well as proof of them being registered with the local environmental health department.

Costs

Be aware of possible hidden costs, such as staffing, table decorations, flowers, etc. Also check out what happens with regard to any breakages of hired items. Asking for an itemised bill prior to your day is a cost-savvy idea.

Guest Numbers

Ask your external caterer if they are prepared to make a visit to your chosen venue, that way you can get their advice regarding numbers – you don't want to over, or under-do your guest numbers.

Menu Ideas

If you've specific ideas about your ideal menu, take these ideas with you to your initial appointments at least then you'll know whether your prospective caterers can accommodate your choices. Ask if the caterer provides mix-and-match menus this can often make your options more interesting and easier to pick.

Negotiation

Wedding caterers, either in-house or external, can sometimes err on the side of being a bit 'tight' when it comes to quantity, so when you're negotiating your food and drinks packages make sure that you go in with a good business head and negotiate hard.

Recommendations

Nobody will give a reference for something as integral as wedding catering, if they've had a bad experience. Ask family, friends or acquaintances who have recently married, for any useful connections or specific recommendations. You could also ask your ceremony/reception venue if there's anyone that they would recommend.

Taste Their Wares!

Before you book an external caterer, or a hotel or restaurant to supply your wedding breakfast and/or buffet – try the food out for yourself. The aesthetics of the venue may look lovely and the menu may sound appealing, but that doesn't guarantee good grub on your plate! And a tasting session is a great way for you and your fiancé to really enjoy this part of your wedding planning.

Florists

Your flowers will play a central role in your wedding day, so choosing the right florist, colour themes, bouquet styles and arrangements will require some careful planning and consideration, from both you and your fiancé.

Your flowers should ultimately complement the ambience of your wedding and more importantly, accentuate the beauty and personality of the bride.

There will be a whole host of different options for you to choose from, which may seem a little daunting when you're first setting out with all your wedding plans. But with the assistance and professional direction of the right florist, you'll find that any concerns will turn rapidly into excitement!

Booking

Start looking for your florist at least 8-10 months before your wedding, especially if you're getting married in peak season. Good florists will be snapped up quickly, so avoid disappointment.

Budget Conscious

Work out a budget for your flowers and communicate it to your florist from the get-go. There's no point in falling in love with a particular choice of florist if their prices are way out of your budget range.

Compare Florists

Meet at least 3 florists and take time to look through their photographic portfolios. Get a feel for how they work, their style and of course, see how competitive their prices are. Ask how long they've been operating for and how many weddings they've done. If you're visiting a florists shop, have a good look at any examples of their creativity on the shop floor.

Delivery

Check where your florist is prepared to deliver to, i.e. will all the flowers be delivered to the venue, or will they deliver to individual names and addresses? You may find that there's a significant difference in pricing for the two different services.

Dress Compatible!

The size, colour and shape of your flowers will have a significant impact on your apparel, so make sure that your bouquet matches your dress and other accessories! Take swatches to your florist appointment, or if you can't get the exact fabric, take something that's very similar in colour – the more detail you can give your florist, the better. If your wedding dress supplier will allow you to take a picture of your dress, take a photo too – if not, you

could perhaps make a rough sketch of the style of the dress. You don't want your flowers to overwhelm your dress but you don't want them to disappear into your dress either. Apply this approach to your bridesmaid's dresses too.

Florist Know-How

Take your florist's advice wherever possible – they're trained in floristry and will have done lots of weddings before. So, if you've fallen in love with a particular table arrangement or bouquet and your florist advises against it, listen to their reasoning and trust their creative insight. Of course, you get the final say, but it's a good idea to sometimes leave it to the experts!

Ideas & Coordination

When visiting prospective florists, take along any ideas, pictures, sketches or other imagery that will help them understand exactly what you want. Lots of information is better than none at all! As an integral part of your day, your flowers should be worked into your chosen theme and the overall mood of your wedding. Talk to your florist about your preferred style, the venue, the season you're getting married in and your wedding party's apparel – anything that will have a bearing on the coordination of your wedding flowers. Check whether your florist would be willing to come out to your venue with you; that way they can really get a feel for the environment and make suggestions related to sizing of arrangements.

Itemised Bill

It's a good idea to have your florist itemise the bill for you, prior to your final flower decisions.

That way you can see your budget in black and white, including any extra expenses such as charges for stands/vases, delivery and collection.

Personality Counts

Your flowers are an integral part of your wedding, so on the run up to your big day you might well want lots of communication with your florist – just checking last minute details. The last thing you want is a supplier who gets shirty with you every time you phone – so make sure that you feel as though you can get on with your florist. If there are any undertones of impatience or wanting to rush you in the early stages, then they're not the florist for you.

Above all, remember that when picking your florist you want someone who is as passionate about making your wedding look gorgeous as you are; someone who will bring creativity, inspiration and expertise to your wedding plans.

Recommendations

Don't underestimate the power of recommendations when choosing your florist – nobody will give a reference for something as integral as wedding floristry, if they've had a bad experience.

Ask family, friends or acquaintances who have recently married, for any useful connections or specific recommendations. If you see some wedding flowers you like, ask who did the flowers. You could also ask your ceremony/reception venue and/or religious minister if there's anyone that they would recommend. Wedding fayres are also a great place for florists to showcase their work.

Seasonal Advice

Any florist worth their salt will be able to advise you on the best seasonal blooms, which will ultimately save you money.

Wedding Flowers to Consider

Bride's Bouquet
Bridesmaid's Bouquets
Flower Girls Flowers/Petals
Special Buttonholes (Groom & Bestman)
Mums' & Grandmothers' Corsages
Ladies' Buttonholes
Gents' Buttonholes
Pedestal Arrangements
Altar/Registrar Table Arrangements
Pew End Arrangements
Archway Arrangements
Candelabra Arrangements
Top Table Arrangements
Reception Table Arrangements
Thank You Bouquets (traditionally for both mums)

Gift Lists

One of the really fun parts of wedding planning; creating your gift list! If you find yourself feeling overwhelmed by any of your wedding plans, then take some time out and go shopping – whether it be a physical trip around a store of your choice, or internet registry – you'll have a ball. That goes for your fiancé too!

Gift Registry

Gone are the days of receiving 3 kettles, 4 toasters and a mismatch of crockery. Wedding gift registries are a free service offered by most large city department stores, providing an opportunity for you and your fiancé to choose the gifts that you would prefer for beginning your married life together.

They also afford a guarantee to your guests that you will actually want the gifts that they have bought for you.

Choosing Your Store

When opting for your choice of gift registry store, first take a look around the store, (or website), and see whether it stocks the type of gifts that appeal to both you and your fiancé. Once you've made your decision you'll be able to contact the store and set up your account. You will then be allocated a sales consultant for your wedding whose services will help guide you through the whole process, from start to finish.

Gift Registry Ideas

Everyday dinnerware
Formal dinnerware
Everyday cutlery
Formal cutlery
Glassware
Electrical goods
Kitchenware & Utensils
Ovenware
Bed linen
Bath linen
Table linen
Luggage
Garden equipment
Outdoor leisure equipment
Home accessories

Honeymoon

It's becoming more popular for couples to ask for a contribution towards their honeymoon, as opposed to the traditional gift giving. This can either be in the form of vouchers, purchased from the travel agents of your choice – or in the form of cash/cheque contribution. You'll need to specify your choice when supplying your gift 'wishes'.

If you feel more comfortable with asking for vouchers, then you'll need to be more organised in terms of timing, i.e. you'll need to have all your vouchers in time for when the balance of your honeymoon is due which is usually some weeks before you're due to go.

Informing Guests

The traditional etiquette for gift lists is for guests to contact the bride's mother or the bridesmaids. However, it's now considered acceptable etiquette for the details of the gift list registry to be included in within the invitations – but not printed on them.

More is Better!

When picking your wedding gifts, always pick more presents than you have guests attending. This gives your guests a greater choice in gifts and price ranges as well as allowing for more than one gift, per guest, to be purchased. It also takes account of anyone who is unable to make it to your wedding, but would like to buy you a gift.

Photography

Often your only tangible visual reminder of the day, having great photographs is a crucial part of your big day. The photographer's role in capturing all your special day's precious, romantic and joyous moments will remain a timeless treasure to you, so finding a professional photographer whose expertise you can trust and rely upon will be of utmost importance.

The right photographer will have the experience, confidence and knowledge to be able to produce professional, quality photographs – even in the most difficult of conditions. So, before you begin your search, take note of some helpful pointers.

Attendant Assistance

On the day, appoint an attendant to help the photographer in identifying who the members of your wedding party are. It will assist timescales and allow your photographer to get the most out of their time with you.

Booking

Book your photographer 8-10 months before your wedding.

Compare Portfolios

Meet at least 3 photographers, (take time to look at their website before you book an appointment, some photography styles will just not be your 'thing'). Take time to look through their portfolios, get a feel to see how competitive their prices are. Liking your photographer and feeling that you'll be able to get on with them will be of paramount importance.

Every Bride's 'Must-Take' Getting Ready Photos

Wedding dress – hanging up, or over a chair
Bride's shoes
Bride's bouquet
Bride having her make-up applied
Bride having her hair done
Bride putting on her garter
Bride in her dress
Close-up of dress details
Bride with bridesmaids
Bride with mum
Bride having finishing touches applied, by bridesmaids and mum
Bride having a pensive moment alone
Full length shot of bride – ready to go!
Bride with dad

Get the Timing Right

To make the most of the time that you have with your photographer and to guarantee the best quality shots, it's a good idea to discuss timings with your photographer and stick to them. That includes when you need to be ready for them, what requested shots you have and how long the photographer feels the whole shoot will take. The last thing you want is to be rushing through your photos due to time constraints.

Personality Counts

If your family and friends are quite rambunctious in nature, it's important that your photographer be confident enough to be able to handle them and 'round-them-up' when needed. So, take account of their disposition when choosing the right photographer for you – you need someone who is confident, composed and in control.

Photographic Styles

Discuss with your fiancé what style of photography you want. For instance, a traditional photography style will focus upon formal line ups, group shots and 'traditional' photographs. Whereas, reportage photography is less formal, taking more impromptu and detailed photographic opportunities. You can opt for a little of both if you'd prefer, but it's best to have an idea before you meet your photographer, so that you can gauge their level of skill in executing a mixture of differing styles.

Think about having a number of black and white photos, within your coloured photography. Black and white photos often look timeless and can really accentuate all the different shades and shapes of your day.

Questions to Ask

Do you shoot using film or a digital camera?
There are pros and cons to both, so if you have a preference, make sure you check this out.

Who will have the copyright to the photographs?
Usually copyright will belong to the photographer, which means that they can use the pictures commercially. Copyright can sometimes be bought after a period of time, but check with your photographer.

How many pictures will you take on the day?
This will depend on whether you've chosen film or digital camera for your shoot – and also on the specific package you're choosing. Be sure to know what you're paying for in terms of numbers taken and the actual numbers of photos included in the package.

How long will you stay on the day?
This will depend very much on what shots you want for your day, (e.g. getting ready, entrance, speeches, etc). Each photographer will have a different way of working, some with loose time limits and others with more rigid time-based packages.

Do we need to provide sustenance for you on the day?
Depending on how long they stay and how they work, your photographer may or may not expect to be fed and watered for your occasion – so it's best to check.

When will I receive my photographs?
Again, this will depend on whether you've digital or film shots, i.e. digital shots will usually be available much sooner, whereas film has to be developed.

Will the photos be accessible on line?
Many friends and family will want to order photographs, so the internet is a great way for them to see all the shots and be able to get their own ordered.

Request List
If you've specific shots that you would like taken on the day, make a list and give this to your photographer taking timings into account.

Reception Music & Entertainment

Your wedding is probably one of the biggest celebrations of your lives and the music and entertainment is a really special way to reflect your feelings of joy and happiness. After months, (and possibly years), of careful planning picking the perfect dress, the most exquisite colour scheme, a picturesque venue, the best food... the last thing that you want is for your entertainment to fall flat on it's face! Your guests will expect a party atmosphere and the opportunity for a bit of a boogie – and your choice of entertainment could make it memorable for either all the right reasons, or for completely the wrong ones. So, here are a few useful pointers for you to start planning your perfect evening of music and entertainment.

'Invite' Suggestions

For a fun and creative way to come up with a playlist ask your guests to come up with a song suggestion in their RSVP – that way you'll get some inspiration and you'll get a broader sense of your guest's music preferences.

First Dance

To get people dancing at the end of your first dance, (rather than having to leave an empty dance floor!), either ask your DJ/band to make an announcement asking the guests to join you on the dance floor for the last few minutes or ask a couple of your close friends and/or

attendants to come up and dance towards the end of the song. Give some thought to the length of your chosen song and make sure that it's not too long; 8-10 minutes might not seem long when you're listening to it at home, but you might regret it halfway through. If your heart is set on the song, then have it cut down to a shorter version – talk to your DJ/band, they should be able to help you decide the right length.

Keep It Varied

You might both be huge fans of 90's rave or 70's disco, but an evening of music filled with nothing but your favourite genre? You're likely to cause a mass exodus! Of course, this is your day, but you've also invited your favoured family and friends to celebrate with you – so be inclusive and give your guests a mixed evening of music, one that everyone can have a dance to. So when you're choosing your playlist, think about older members of the family, as well as your own generation – throw in the odd 'swing' number or a bit of jazz; whatever will get your Great Uncle Chas doing his thing on the dance floor!

Live Music

If you opt for live music at your reception, bear in mind that they'll need to take breaks during the evening so you'll either need a DJ to fill the gaps, or an iPod or CD with a selection of music that your guests can dance to.

Music & Mood

If you're planning on music playing through your sit down meal, make sure that it's appropriate for the moment! You may be a huge rock or hip hop fan, but blaring out Iron Maiden or Eminem during your meal isn't likely to aid digestion, or conversation! Stick to low key instrumentals or soft ballads for a more dinner-friendly mood.

Other Entertainment

Of course, you don't have to stick to the traditional concept of a wedding DJ or band. You might want music, accompanied by other entertainment styles, such as magicians, jugglers, children's entertainers, face painting, belly-dancers, salsa dancers and instructors, themed displays… whatever tickles your entertainment fancy!

Song Lyrics

Naturally, you'll want to play music to your taste but you'll also need to keep in mind to weed out song choices which contain explicit lyrics or adult themes. You might like the idea of seeing your sour-puss Aunty Brenda's face as she listens to toe-curling lyrics, but is it worth upsetting other older members of your wedding party? Not to mention those with children. Keep it clean and avoid the risk of offending your nearest and dearest.

Sound Check!

There shouldn't be any non-resolvable sound issues with your chosen live entertainment, but if your venue is in a remote outdoor location, ensure that it doesn't turn out to be an acoustic nightmare, e.g. waves, wind, trees etc. Discuss this with your choice of entertainment before you make a booking, as they should be able to identify any possible acoustic limitations.

Take Some Control

Your DJ might have come recommended to you, but don't allow yourself to be lured into a false sense of security. A great playlist to one person may end up being your idea of a musical nightmare – so be sure to make a list of your own playlist requests and even add in some 'absolutely don't plays'!

Volume Control

Despite the fact that it's a celebration, club-like volume will not go down well with the older members of your wedding it'll also make it virtually impossible for your guests to talk.

Popular First Dance Songs

Always	Atlantic Star
Amazed	Lonestar
Chasing Cars	Snow Patrol
Don't Know Much	Aaron Neville & Linda Ronstadt
Don't Wanna Miss a Thing	Aerosmith
Endless Love	Diana Ross & Lionel Richie
First Time Ever I Saw Your Face	Roberta Flack
From This Moment	Shania Twain
Have I Told You Lately	Rod Stewart
(I've Had) The Time of My Life	Jennifer Warnes & Bill Medley
She's The One	Robbie Williams
The Air That I Breathe	Hollies
The Way You Look Tonight	Tony Bennett / Steve Tyrell
Up Where We Belong	Jennifer Warnes & Joe Cocker
We've Only Just Begun	Carpenters
When a Man Loves a Woman	Percy Sledge
Wonderful Tonight	Eric Clapton
You Do Something to Me	Paul Weller
You Raise Me Up	Westlife

Transport
Visual Check
Whether you're having a vintage car, coach and horses or a stretched limo for your wedding transport make sure that you ask to see what you're renting before you commit to a booking. Check the vehicles both inside and out, ensuring that they're in a good state of repair, clean and that your dress will fit inside. Also ask the owner to confirm that the vehicles that you have checked over will be the ones that turn up on the day.

Itemised Bill
Request an itemised bill, prior to booking.

Wedding Stationery
As the first contact with your guests, you'll want your invitations to reflect the mood and style of your wedding. Picking the right stationery will be a highly personal choice for you and your fiancé so it is important that you take time to consider your choices.

Over-Order
Order 35-40 more invitations and envelopes than you think you need - but remember to take into account that you only need 1 invite per couple or per family. It's cheaper to over-order as part of your main order, than to re-order a smaller amount later on.

You can be guaranteed that between 10%-35% of your initial guest list won't be able to attend, so you may have people that you would like to invite in their place. This also allows for mistakes when you're writing out your invitations.

Proof Read

If you're choosing to have your wedding invitations printed by professional stationers, always get a sample of your invitations before you give them the final go-ahead. Check the proof thoroughly, making sure that there are no printing or time, date, venue errors. Ask a friend to double check, just to make sure that you're not reading what you think it should read.

Stationery Needs to Consider

Ceremony & Wedding Breakfast Invitations
Evening Reception Invitations
Reply Cards
Order of Service
Menus
Place Cards
Thank You Cards

Don't forget your 'thank you' cards! After the months of organising prior to your wedding, you'll no doubt want to sit-back and relax, so forgetting about your cards will be all too easy. The best way to ensure that your memory doesn't lapse is to order them with your invitations – that way they'll match your other stationery too.

Wedding Resources

Accessories

www.accessoriesofdistinction.co.uk
www.confetti.co.uk
www.therealprincesscompany.com
www.theweddingveilshop.co.uk
www.wedoweddingaccessories.co.uk

Religious Organisations & Officiants

Baptist Union of Great Britain
www.baptist.org.uk

British Humanist Association
www.humanism.org.uk

Church of England
www.cofr.anglican.org

Church of Scotland
www.churchofscotland.org.uk

General Register Office
www.gro.gov.uk

General Register Office for Scotland
www.gro-scotland.gov.uk

Jewish Marriage Council
www.jmc-uk.org

Dresses

www.almostnewweddingdresses.co.uk
www.bridaldesigner.co.uk
www.designerbridalroom.com

Honeymoons & Weddings Abroad

www.kuoni.co.uk/weddings
www.weddingsabroad.com
www.whitesandweddings.co.uk

Invitations

www.brideandgroomdirect.co.uk

General Wedding Internet Sites

www.findaweddingsupplier.co.uk
www.frugalbride.com
www.hitched.co.uk
www.loveweddings.co.uk
www.newlyweds-uk.com
www.onewedding.co.uk
www.thebridalwearcompany.co.uk
www.theweddingshop.co.uk
www.weddingchannel.com
www.weddingchaos.co.uk
www.weddingdiaries.co.uk
www.wedding-directories.com
www.weddings.co.uk
www.wedfrugal.com
www.weddingguideuk.com
www.yourukwedding.com

Magazines

www.bridesmagazine.co.uk
www.weddingmagazine.co.uk
www.weddingideasmagazine.co.uk
www.youandyourwedding.co.uk

Wedding Shows & Exhibitions

www.bridaldesigner.co.uk
www.designerweddingshow.co.uk
www.nationalweddingshow.co.uk
www.theukweddingshows.co.uk

Wedding Experiences

www.wedding-experience.co.uk

Bridal Wear & Beauty

Bridal Wear

The time is here… the time to tap into your inner Princess and find your dream wedding dress! If you've never snuck into a bridal shop and pretended you're engaged, then chances are that this will be a totally new experience for you.

You will likely be purchasing the most expensive item of clothing you're ever going to wear – all for one day! So you're going to need plenty of support, advice and positive feedback in choosing the right dress for you. There are literally hundreds upon hundreds of glamorous, exquisite and beautiful dresses out there for you to try on so you're guaranteed plenty of choice in your search for 'the one'.

Alterations

The vast majority of dresses are made in standard sizes, (which will vary from designer to designer), so it's unlikely that you'll have a perfect fit once your chosen dress arrives. Most dresses will need alteration, so don't be surprised or worry about it.

Appointments

Most wedding stores and salons now require you to make an appointment to come and look at their wedding dresses. The downside being that you can't just walk off the street into a shop, but the upside being that you'll have time to rally your closest friends/family to help you and you'll have the assistant's time and attention rather than having to vie with other brides-to-be. Be sure to cancel in plenty of time if you can't make it.

Assistants & Personal Space

If you've never tried a dress on before, then the up-close-and-personal nature of the assistants may come as a bit of a shock. Most will come into the changing room and help you get into your dress although they'll usually wait for you to tell them that you're ready for them.

Remember that they're there to look after the stock, as well as attend to and look after you. Enjoy the attention - it's probably one of the last times anyone will want to help dress you!

However, if you're really not happy about such attention, then mention it to your assistant and ask to come to some compromise, so that they can do their job and you can retain your personal space.

Attendant Help
Whatever you do, don't forget to take one or two of your attendants with you to your dress fittings. They will need to learn how to help you in and out of your dress, how to tie corset backs and operate complicated straps, how to bustle your dress and how to get rid of any seating 'wrinkles'.

Beauty Vs Comfort
It's no good having stunning beauty on the day if you feel like the bodice on your dress is going to crush your lungs, like your feet are going to explode from pain and like you can't stop tripping over your extra-long veil when you're dancing. Looking and feeling gorgeous is a must, of course – but it needs to be balanced with your comfort, (not to mention your health and safety!). So pick something that combines your idea of beauty with what you also feel comfortable and can move freely in. You want to feel great on the day, not have your face contorted in agony. Not a good look for your photos…

Be Prepared
Heaven forbid that something happen to the dress on the day of the wedding – a stubborn crease, a mystery mark or a spillage… it's best to at least know how to treat any mishap, rather than go into a flat-spin panic on the day of your wedding. You won't be jinxing yourself by asking, so take the time to check with your dress supplier for any do's and don'ts and/or useful products you can use.

Beware! Cheap Imitations

If you choose to buy your dress from an unknown internet source or have a design duplicated, then you are potentially taking a risk. It doesn't mean that it won't be successful, but think carefully about putting yourself in such a vulnerable position. Bearing in mind that different fabrics are likely to be used, which will change the drop and shape of the dress.

Body Shape

We're not all blessed with TV-guru-style knowledge when it comes to what body shape we are and what suits us, so if you're not sure, get some advice. Knowing your body shape will steer you away from things that won't suit you and you'll be confident in what does suit you.

Bring Your Ideas

You might have a very clear picture of the sort of dress you want, but even if you profess not to have a clue, I bet you'll know exactly what you don't like! Before you start shopping, think about what you'd like – modern, simple, traditional, sleeved, off-the-shoulder, fishtail… if you change your mind once you start trying dresses on, at least you'll have a starting point.

Budget

If you don't have a designer budget, don't try on a designer dress! Simple. If a dress is out of your price range, put it straight back onto the rail. Don't be talked into 'just trying it on' by unscrupulous assistants who are already aware of your budget restrictions.

Compare Prices

When comparing dresses from different stores, you will need to factor in any additional services or costs, e.g. does the store charge extra for each fitting, and if so, how much?

Deposit

Once you've chosen your dress, be prepared to pay anything up to 50% as a deposit – with the remaining balance due once the dress arrives. Once you've committed to the sale, there's no going back on it.

Diet Plans

You might well intend to lose weight for your wedding day, but DON'T be tempted to buy a dress smaller than the size you are when you order it. You might think it's the ultimate incentive – but what if you don't, or can't lose the weight? It's easy to take a dress in, but it's a much more complicated and expensive exercise to have to take a dress out, or at worst, it's just impossible. It's not worth the risk.

Early Starters

Some brides begin looking and buying ultra-early, (some 18-24 months beforehand), which is all well and good for organisational purposes, but do bear in mind that you'll be narrowing down future seasonal 'new additions' to wedding dress collections. It's great fun to start looking as soon as you're engaged, so let yourself go and enjoy the process – but if you're one for wanting to be up-to-date with seasonal fashions, resist the urge to buy too early. Usually 8-10 months before your wedding is a reasonable timescale within which to work keeping in mind that dresses need to be ordered which can take 4-6 months, plus time for fittings and any alterations.

Emotions

The process of finding your wedding dress will be a mixture of fun, exhilaration and girly-bonding! But alongside this, you may well also feel a little overwhelmed and stressed at times. Be reassured that all these emotions are completely normal and to be expected. Your dress is a pivotal representative of your wedding, so of course it's an emotive time for you.

Fitting Guide

When your dress arrives and you finally have your fitting, here are a few pointers to help ensure that any alteration needs are accurately recorded.

Ensure that you can move comfortably - sitting, walking, arms up in the air!

Check for any obvious pulling, wrinkling or uncomfortable bunching.

Check that the dress stays in place as you move around - slipping down is not an option!

Check that the hem of a full-length dress just touches the tops of your toes. Schedule more fittings until you're happy with the fit of your dress - this is not the time to be coy about things you're not happy with.

Independent Salons

Chain stores can be great for easy access, but smaller more independent stores will often provide a larger range of styles, designers and more intimate service.

Larger Sizes

Some manufacturers charge extra for larger dress sizes, so make sure that you check this out with your supplier before ordering.

No Children Allowed

Whether you, or your friends, have children – they should not go with you when looking for dresses. They could cause damage to the dresses, costing you money and no matter how well behaved they usually are, boredom will kick in and at best, you'll be distracted and at worst, you'll be totally mortified by their behaviour.

No Regrets

Once you've picked your dress, stop looking! Don't try on any other dresses and don't torture yourself with flipping through magazines and websites, wondering "What if...?".

Operation Dress-Shopping

It's not just as simple as strolling up on the day to try on lots of dresses, oh no... firstly, there are a few pre-trying-on rules to remember:-

Check with the retailer whether you need an appointment to try on dresses.

Make sure you're showered, hair-washed and zinging with cleanliness.

Don't wear your trusty 'comfy' shoes if when you remove them they're smelly.

Avoid hand and body lotion, unless you can leave it a few hours before your appointment. It could leave an oily residue on the dresses.

Don't apply false tan – it could ruin gowns and you won't get a proper sense of what colours suit you.

Avoid too much make-up, especially foundation and blushers. That'll stop you covering the dresses with 'feint beige' or 'summer bronze'. It'll also help find shades/colours that suit your complexion.

Clean underwear – but not a thong – is a must.

Keep jewellery simple, or don't wear it at all. You don't want any snagging disasters. If you're adamant you want to wear jewellery, ask one of your friends to hold it for you whilst you're donning your dress choices.

Price Tags Vs The Dress

So, your best mate's dress cost her over a month's salary - do you need to compete? Dresses from top designer outlets will have you believing that your day is dependant on a particular price tag, rather than the dress itself. Of course, there are some beautiful designer dresses out there, but there are also many, many more available at a more reasonable price. You want something that flatters you and your personality - something that will make your groom beam with happiness and pride as he sees you. You want everyone to notice how gorgeous you look, not just your dress.

Shoes

Finding the right shoes will be as integral as finding the right dress, certainly in terms of comfort. Unless you're a pro at wearing very high heels for long periods, stick with low or medium height heels. You'll be on your feet for a very long time, so blisters and aching feet will not be conducive to a happy, smiling bride!

Sizing

Don't be disheartened by the sizing structures of wedding dresses; they don't reflect the normal sizing guides that we're used to with everyday clothes. So if you're normally a size 12 and your wedding dress is a size 16, you haven't suddenly gained two dress sizes in weight, it's just the way that wedding dresses are sized. Phew!

Too Many Cooks...

Shopping for your dress is a wonderful experience, but it's also deeply personal. It's great fun to take a lot of girly-friends, but you run the risk of being incorrectly influenced (or just downright confused!). Choose instead either one or two close, trusted friends whose opinion you respect and who will be honest and objective with you.

Wedding Beauty

You're getting married, so of course, you want and deserve to be the most beautiful and glamorous version of you for your day. Enhancing your own personal beauty will make you feel wonderfully polished, confident and relaxed – and it'll shine through for all to see in your self-assured smile, poise and happiness. Here are some great hints and tips to make all your beauty dreams come true, making sure that you look and feel fabulous for one of the most important days of your life.

Body Care

Treat yourself to a good skin care routine and a good body scrub. Be sure to pay special attention to your neck, chest and arms – especially if you have an off-the-shoulder or strapless dress. Invest in a good quality natural bristle dry body brush and use it daily. Dry brushing is a care regime, which works in assisting the body eliminate toxins through the skin, stimulating blood circulation and the lymphatic system and improving the distribution of fat deposits in the body. It also feels great! Make a habit of dry brushing before you shower, it'll really wake you up and you'll see the benefits within weeks. Get into a good moisturising routine in the months running up to your wedding. Well moisturised skin will show, so don't leave this important beauty factor until a few days before. A good body massage can do your skin the world of good, as well as calming your nerves! It'll stimulate your circulation, soothe your muscles and make you feel like a million dollars!

Exercise!

Even if you're not trying to lose a bit of weight before your wedding, exercise will help to tone up your skin, as well as giving your circulation a boost and giving you a great healthy looking glow.

Alabaster or golden glow?

If you're feeling a little pale and pasty, test out a fake tan a few weeks before your wedding, opting for one suited to your skin tone – this may be a little trial and error, so give yourself plenty of time to avoid any orange-embarrassments on the day! If you're unsure, there are plenty of in-store beauty consultants who will be able to help you – or you could opt for a professional spray tan by a professional beautician.

Facial Skin Care

First and foremost, concentrate on establishing and maintaining a good cleansing routine on the run up to your wedding. It's no good spending the earth on cover-sticks and foundations to cover up imperfections, if your facial care routine is at the core of any issues you may have. Of course, good base make-up is important, but the more of a natural glow your skin has, the better.

What you put into your body is as important as what you put onto it! Your diet will be an integral part of achieving a healthy, glowing complexion for your big day. So plenty of fruit and vegetables and lots of water. Give your system the best chance it has to do you proud.

Drink up to 8 glasses of water per day; this will prevent your skin from becoming dehydrated, as well as aiding the elimination of toxins from your body, which will help reduce spots.

Be vigilant about touching your skin too much, as this will spread bacteria from your hands onto your face. You might be tempted to touch your face more if you're feeling stressed, so just be aware.

Smoking is a sure-fire way to dehydrate your skin. It also destroys collagen, speeding up the aging process. Stopping completely is the best cure, but if you can't, at least cut down.

Don't squeeze any spots in the days/weeks before your wedding. You'll either cause scarring or you'll infect the area with more bacteria, making your spots worse. If you've a spot that's come to a head on the day of your wedding, very gently, roll it between two clean fingers until the centre comes out. If you've a red spot that's not 'ready' DO NOT attempt to squeeze it, you'll just end up with an inflamed red lump.

Sleep, sleep and more sleep! Of course, you'll have lots to do on the run up to your wedding, but where possible relax and invest in having lots of early nights. It's no good burning the candle at both ends and then having an early night the night before your wedding – long term tiredness will show in your face.

If you're unfortunate enough to be bothered by skin problems, such as acne, see your GP well in advance of your wedding, (preferably 6-12 months). They will either be able to prescribe you with medication to help your skin, or refer you to a dermatologist for a consultation. If you've a generous budget, then treat yourself to professional skin treatments and take the time to consult with your preferred salon and find out what best suits your skin. If, on the other hand, you've a more limited budget, do a little homework in beauty magazines as there are some great products out there, which won't break the bank.

Microdermabrasion products are a fabulous way to exfoliate your skin, giving your skin a more natural glow; they also work to fade pigmentation marks and other surface imperfections. But make sure that you carefully follow the instructions on the packaging, as overuse, or immediate exposure to the sun can cause dermatological problems.

Investing in a good facial massage can improve the look of your skin by boosting circulation and stimulating your body's natural lymphatic drainage processes, which will decrease puffiness and give your skin a gorgeous radiant look. Test any new product well before your wedding day, just to check that your skin doesn't have an adverse reaction to it. Eye creams can be a bit hit and miss, as this is often the most sensitive area of your face. The last thing you want is a break out of spots or puffy, dry eyes on your special day.

If you wake up on the day and you've hardly slept leaving you with puffy eyes don't despair – the old remedies are often the best. A slice of cold cucumber on each of your eyes for a few minutes will help cool the eyes and leave them feeling refreshed. Or, try wrapping some frozen peas in a cloth and place them over your eyes, again cooling them and reducing the puffiness. If your eyes are looking tired or a little bloodshot on the day, pop in a couple of eye drops, but make sure that it's one that you've used before – just in case of irritation or allergic reaction.

If your teeth could do with a little brightening, you don't have to spend a fortune having specialist dental treatments – there are plenty of over-the-counter teeth brightening products that will put the sparkle back into your smile.

Foot Care

With all the other beauty 'demands' it would be easy to forget your feet, but a little bit of nail polish is not going to cut it if you're wearing open toed shoes on your big day. And even if you're not, your honeymoon is likely to require lots of sandal-action, whilst you're taking romantic strolls with your new hubby, so the last thing you want is dry, knobbly or gnarled feet! Time for some foot TLC!

If your feet are generally neglected, (i.e. you've pretty much never, or very rarely, bothered treating them), then you're probably better off initially seeing a podiatrist. They will be able to concentrate on getting rid of dry, cracked or rough skin and any unsightly calluses or knobbles.

Once you've seen a podiatrist, or if your feet are in generally good shape anyway, book into see a pedicurist. This treatment will be a real pamper for your feet, usually with a relaxing foot soak, buffing treatment, scented softening creams and professional toenail clipping, trimming and painting. Fit for a wedding Princess!

Hair

Don't leave your hair to chance on the day and wing it with a home cut and colour! Nothing less than a professional stylist will do for your special day. After all… You're worth it! On the run-up to your wedding, invest in some weekly intensive conditioning treatments and keep up to date with your hair cuts and colours. You might want longer locks for the big day, but split ends will make your hair look shorter than it is – and straggly to boot. Not a good look!

If your hair is in dire need of some TLC, pop into your local salon for information on hair treatments. They'll be able to give you specific advice on hair/scalp problems and provide you with products that will cost less than you think.

You want to feel like a polished version of 'you' on the day, not someone completely different. So, when choosing your hairstyle of the day, try not to change your look too drastically. For instance, you might like an up-do when you have your trial, but if it's not how you usually wear your hair, think carefully about whether you'd be in your comfort zone for the whole day.

Book at least 3 trials for your hairstyle a few months before you're wedding; it's crucial that your crowning glory has the best style and right stylist for the job. Try to avoid any style which is too trendy, it might look great on the day, but it might date easily, making your wedding photos a source of embarrassment, rather than of pleasure. Discuss any hair accessories with your stylist and take along pictures of your dress and any ideas that you may have. Your last trial before the day should involve using the actual accessories for the day. Avoid any disappointments and upset and pre-book your stylist well in advance.

Prepare your hair for the day by using a good conditioning product and deep-penetrating hair treatments for at least 2-3 weeks before your wedding. If you're wearing a veil and intend to remove it after the ceremony, ask your hairdresser to ask your maid of honour, your mum or your sister, how to remove it without causing your hair-do to collapse.

Hand Care

Your hands will be a major feature of your day; exchanging rings, with everyone wanting to take a peak at your wedding ring, greeting your guests, signing the register, throwing your bouquet, as well as holding hands with your new husband – so you'll want them to look and feel beautiful.

Start your hand care routine 3-6 months before your wedding, keeping your hands and nail beds well moisturised. If you don't already, always wear gloves for housework and washing dishes. This will protect your hands and nails from harsh household products and drying. If you're lucky enough to be able to grow your own beautiful nails for the day, invest in a good cuticle cream, keeping them soft and supple for healthy nail growth.

Make an appointment for a full treatment manicure, including a hand exfoliation, deep cleansing and moisturising treatment and nail filing/shaping. If you're opting for a set of nail tips or false nails for your day, it's worth having a trial, so that you can see what shape you like, how they feel and how quickly they come off. Book your trial appointment a few months ahead and don't forget to book in for the day before your big day. A quick word on dressing if you have false nail tips… if you've a complicated dress, make sure that someone can help you in and out of it on the day - the last thing you need is a button left undone or worse a nail coming off!

Make-Up

If you've any doubts about what make-up to buy, or if you want a different look for your special day, head to your local department store and approach the make-up consultants for help and advice. Some cosmetic companies will even give you a 'bridal makeover' so you can see the products actually on you – and get a serious pampering at the same time! Make sure to remember that you'll need to coordinate your make-up with your personal colour scheme for the day – as well as it suiting your skin tone.

Pick your make-up products early and practice with them. Try out a few different 'looks' and settle on the one that you're most comfortable with. Don't be to 'out there' in your choice of make-up style, try going for something that will stand the test of time in your wedding photos. Invest in good quality make-up and test products before the day, (to make sure you have no surprise allergic reactions). Better quality products will last longer.

When applying your make-up, natural daylight is always best. If at all possible, set up a mirror near a window, with the light shining directly onto your face, not from behind or to the side of you. Naturally, you want your make-up to last, but rather than apply heavy foundation over your whole face, try targeting strategic areas with concealer, (under the eyes, over blemishes, etc), and then applying your foundation over the top.

Use a tinted foundation with an SPF, especially if you're getting married outdoors. You'll be in the sunshine for longer than it will feel, so protect your skin.

Take your lipstick with you on the day, as that will be the one thing that you'll need to keep reapplying!

Wear waterproof mascara! Nothing else will do. Whether it's a few tears or the equivalent of Niagara Falls, you really don't want the streaked-panda look on your wedding day. If you're concerned about your mascara running on the day, or even whilst you're swimming in the pool/sea on your honeymoon try an eyelash tint and perm. This process will curl and colour lashes, making them more defined – with no mascara nightmares. A trial treatment is a must, some weeks before your wedding.

If you're using bronzer on your face, don't forget your neck and shoulders. Two-tone might be your theme, but it's not a good make-up look. Watch where your dress comes to though, you don't want it to stain.

Invest in buying good make-up tools – you might not think that they make that much difference, but they're essential. Train yourself to understand that what you apply your make-up with is as important as what you apply. No good buying an expensive killer-blusher if you don't have the right brush to apply it with.

You could choose to employ a make-up artist for your wedding make-up although there are obvious costs involved. They are professionally trained and will ultimately save you money on expensive make-up products for the day. If you decide on this route, it's important that you have an idea of what YOU want to look like and for you to communicate this very clearly to your make-up artist. You want to feel like a more pampered and glowing version of you on the day and not as though the body snatchers have been in and replaced you with an unrecognisable face!

Many make-up artists will tell you that your make-up needs to be heavier for your wedding photos which in essence is true but don't feel pushed into wearing make-up that feels too heavy for you. The most important thing for you is to feel comfortable with yourself, that way your own natural confidence will transfer into your pictures – far more important than being able to see your eyeliner!

Spread the cost of expensive, luxury make-up and skin care items by sharing them with your bridesmaids, sisters or mum – this will mean that you can all afford to look and feel fantastic as well as being co-ordinated!

The Bride

Venues

The Bride

Ceremony & Reception Venues

Arguably, the most important decision you'll make for your wedding day, your ceremony and reception venue choice can leave any bride-and-groom-to-be feeling a little anxious. But the reality is that there are a world of wonderful choices available for your perfect day whether it be a church, a registry office, a castle, a village hall or even a tropical beach. Often considered as the pivotal starting point to planning your whole wedding, once you've chosen and secured your venue(s), you can get on with the rest of your sourcing and organising, working your theme and style into the setting of your venue(s). But before you book any viewing appointments, here are a few pointers to help you on your way.

The Ceremony

Although this part of the day is fulfilling your legal obligations in order to be married, the ceremony is the most special and meaningful part of your wedding day. This marks the point at which you both vow to be together for the rest of your lives, declaring your enduring love, commitment and respect for each other. As the very beginning of your married life, your family and friends are there to both witness and celebrate your union, so the room in which your ceremony takes place is going to have a special place in your heart for the rest of your lives. Choosing it well will make it especially memorable.

The Reception

Whether you're having a smaller day reception and a larger evening reception or an all day reception with the same number of guests, this part of the celebrations is your first formal introduction as husband and wife. Your reception is the time to let your hair down and have a great party with all your nearest and dearest – this is one of the most joyous days of your lives, so your reception venue is another important, but highly personal, choice. Don't get hung up on glossy magazines and other people's view of what your reception should look like - what do you and your fiancé want? And what does you budget allow? Be it a glamorous 5-course dinner and formal dance in a stately home, a sophisticated cocktail party, a buffet in a village hall, an afternoon knees-up in the local pub or a huge marquee in sprawling grounds... it's your idea of 'wonderful' that counts.

A1 Venue Checklist – 'Must-Ask' Questions

Book your venue as soon as possible, popular venues can be booked up to 2 years in advance!

First and foremost, is the venue available on your chosen date? Check this before you make an appointment – you don't want a wasted journey, especially if your date is non-negotiable.

Is the price of the venue within your allocated budget?

Is your venue big enough to accommodate your intended guest list?

If your ceremony and reception venue are in different places, are they near to each other? What practical transport issues might any distance pose? And how will this affect the enjoyment of yours and your guest's day?

Will there be any other weddings held on the same day? If so, what is the distance apart in terms of timing? Remember that your cake and flower suppliers will need to arrive earlier – so you don't want any unnecessary delays.

If your venue has accommodation, will your guests receive any discount? What number of rooms will be held for your wedding and how long for?

Will your venue(s) accommodate your choice of entertainment, decoration and any other themed ideas?

If you have any members of your wedding party with mobility difficulties, how will the venue(s) accommodate this? Make sure that you also check outside the venue, there may be cobbles, steps or slopes which may cause problems.

Does your venue have a licence to sell alcohol? Is there any flexibility with regards to bar closing times?

Will you be allowed to move any pictures and other furnishings to allow for your own choices of decoration?

Are there any noise pollution regulations in the area where your venue is located? You might want to party until the early hours and your entertainment may have to stop at midnight.

Do your venue quotes include VAT, any service charges or booking fees? Request a clear breakdown of costs – you don't want to find out after the fact that linen, bar staff, waiters and crockery weren't in the original quote.

How much will your deposit be and is it refundable?

What is the venue's cancellation policy?

Is there a minimum fee for the venue? Some venues will charge for all facilities, even if you don't use them – especially if you have exclusivity on the day.

If your wedding breakfast is being held in a restaurant, will you have the room exclusively for the duration?

Be Flexible

If you've set your heart on a particular venue and it's booked on your chosen date, then allow yourself to consider alternative dates. If it's a popular peak season venue, then chances are that you could have a wait on your hands – so think about picking a Friday, or other weekday. As long as you can give your guests enough notice, those most important to you will be happy to book a day's holiday to celebrate your wedding.

Contracts

Once you've chosen your venue, make sure that you have all the necessary details included within your contract and always check over the 'small print' before you sign. Better to be safe, than tearing your hair out because of some missed detail, or unexpected contractual hitch.

Humanist Ceremonies

If you'd like to hold a ceremony which is not restricted in terms of your beliefs, personality, location and overall ambience you could opt for a Humanist ceremony. This could then be followed by a celebration befitting your personal preferences. A Humanist ceremony isn't recognised as a legal marriage, so you should also officially marry at a registry office, (before or after your ceremony).

Location, Location, Location!

If you and your fiancé are from different towns, counties or even countries, choosing an ideal venue location can be a tad tricky, (not to mention political!). There are a few ways in which you can tackle this etiquette issue - one is to find a neutral location which is somewhere in between both family locations; preferably as equidistant as possible. But if the distance between the two is too great for this to be practicable, then perhaps one family could play 'host' to the other family. Obviously, this will

depend on your families' personalities and preferences, so talk through your options with all involved.

Overseas Weddings

If your preference is to marry abroad, it's likely that only a relatively small number of family and friends will be able to make the journey. If you feel you'd like to celebrate with a wider number of people, you could perhaps throw a wedding celebration party on your return.

Plan B

If you choose a predominantly outdoor event, you'll need a 'Plan B'... just in case the heaven's open. Make sure that your venue can accommodate a sudden need for cover!

Priorities

Work out with your fiancé what your joint priorities are in terms of your dream wedding day. This will help you to shape an idea of what style, size and location of venue you want. Start with questions such as:-

Do you want a formal or relaxed atmosphere?
Do you want to get married indoors or outdoors?
Do you want a small or large guest list?
Do you want to get married abroad, or at home?
Do you want to be as near to both families as possible?
Do you want tasteful modern settings, or something more olde-worlde with character?
Do you want an unusual venue, with a real 'wow-factor'?
Do you want a civil or religious ceremony?

Each question will assist you in narrowing down the type of venue for you.

Recommendations

Nobody will give a good reference for something as integral as a wedding venue, if they've had a bad experience. Ask family, friends or acquaintances who have recently married, for any useful connections or specific recommendations. You can also check out wedding forums for more information on potential venues.

Research

Rather than making countless trips around potential venues, do some research on the internet before stepping out your front door. Source venue websites, testimonials, forums and request brochures. Most venues will provide a reasonably comprehensive information pack, from which you can shortlist your favourites.

Seasonal Choices

Depending on the time of year, your venue choice may be best served reflecting the season you've chosen to marry in. For example, beautifully landscaped gardens and waterfalls will be better in the summer months whereas grand halls and roaring fireplaces will be more suited to winter weddings.

Traditions, Roles & Etiquette

Traditions, Roles and Etiquette

Attendants

On your wedding day, you and your groom should be free to focus on each other and enjoy every precious minute of this magical day. So, with so much for you to plan, do and think about in the run-up, you'll be in need of some special help and attention before, during and after the wedding. Attendants play an integral part in assisting organisational plans, in paying attention to finer detail and most importantly of all, providing love, friendship, honesty and invaluable support at a crucial time.

Attendants and Their Duties

Maid/Matron of Honour or Chief Bridesmaid

There are different schools of thought in relation to whether the term is coined correctly as Maid/Matron of Honour or Chief Bridesmaid – but essentially they do the same thing, i.e. they are the Bride's right-hand-woman! A Maid of Honour is traditionally a single female, who has not been married whereas the Matron of Honour is a female who either is, or has been married. In the spirit of being politically correct, Chief Bridesmaid lends itself as a 'covers-all' name, in that it makes no reference to the attendant's marital status. Whichever term you choose to use, whoever takes this role is essentially the main 'attendant' of the Bride. Typically, the role is afforded to an adult, female family member or best friend. Traditional duties encompass the following:-

Before the day

Accompanying the Bride with shopping for her dress, shoes, lingerie, accessories, etc – providing honest feedback and ideas.

Assist with making/organising wedding favours.

Assist with writing invitations.

Hosting a 'bridal shower'.

Help in choosing Bridesmaids outfits.

Notifying other female attendants of rehearsal dates and times.

Planning and organising the 'hen-party' including the invitation of guests.

Arranging fittings for other female attendant's dresses, delivery and pick-ups.

On the day

Helping to 'dress' the Bride on the day.

Helping keep the Bride on schedule.

Accompanying the Bride to the ceremony location.

Arranging the Bride's veil and train before she proceeds down the aisle (carrying it if necessary).

Holding the groom's ring before the exchange of rings.

Taking the Bride's Bouquet during the ceremony, returning it after the bride and groom share their first kiss.

Takes care of the Bride's personal effects at the ceremony and reception.

Organising and co-ordinating the other Bridesmaids and child attendants.

Signing the register as a legal witness.

Offering a toast at the reception.

Assisting the Bride with 'bustling' her dress for the reception.

Accompanying the bride to the bathroom!

Dancing with the Best Man.

Assisting the Bride in changing and storing her dress, if she is going away.

Gathering special mementos for the Bride; guest book, disposable cameras, cake topping, etc.

Looking after the safe transportation of gifts, if the Bride is going away.

Bridesmaids

Before the day

Assisting the Bride with pre-wedding errands.

Attending dress fittings.

Attending rehearsals.

Attending pre-wedding celebrations.

On the day

Walking in procession down the aisle, behind the Bride.

Sitting at the Bridal table.

Caring for child attendants.

Helping with practical preparations at the reception.

Best Man

Acting as the Groom's chief male attendant the Best Man assumes responsibility for various organisational aspects of the day, as well as supporting and assisting the Groom. Traditional duties include:-

Before the day

Assisting the Groom with shopping for Morning Suit, rings, gifts, etc.
Organise transport for guests from the ceremony to the reception venue.
Arranging fittings for other male attendant's suits, delivery and pick-ups.
Notifying other male attendants of rehearsal dates and times.
Planning and organising the 'stag-do' including the invitation of guests.
Assisting in making reservations for the Groom's family and out-of-town guests for overnight accommodation.

On the day

Assisting the Groom in getting ready, (including calming any frayed nerves!).
Drive the Groom to the ceremony location on time.
Supervising buttonholes and Orders of Service.
Looking after the Bride's ring before the exchange of rings.
Organising the Ushers and any other male attendants on the day.
Signing the register as a legal witness.
Organising the Groom's going-away clothes, if required.
Providing the relevant Officiant with their fee.
Liaise with a Toastmaster for timings of speeches, card reading, cake cutting, etc; or, acting as Toastmaster.
Making the first toast to the Bride and Groom.
Escorting the Maid/Matron of Honour in the ceremony and reception.
Looking after the Groom's personal effects during the ceremony and reception.
Dancing with the Maid/Matron of Honour.
Making a speech at the Wedding Breakfast, including cards and telegrams.
Dancing with the Bride and other female attendants.
Taking the Bride and Groom's luggage to the car or hotel room.
Assisting with the transportation of wedding gifts.
Making sure that the car is ready for the Bride and Groom to leave the reception.
Returning the Groom's suit and other male attendants suits to the hire company.

Groomsmen and Ushers

Assisting the Groom and Best Man with errands before the wedding.

Attending suit fittings.

Attending rehearsals.

Assistance with seating plans.

Escorting guests to their seats at the ceremony (Bride: left, Groom: right)

Seating the Groom's parents and Bride's mother at the front.

Placing aisle-runner in place, after all of the guests have arrived and before the Bride begins her entrance. Taking up the runner at the end.

Guiding the guests out of the ceremony and to the reception.

Escorting the Bridesmaids out of the ceremony.

Direct guests to the appropriate facilities at the reception.

Dancing with the Bridesmaids at the reception.

Flower Girls

Flower girls are usually female child attendants, between the ages of 4 and 10 years. Their role is to precede the bride, tossing petals in the path of the bride's entrance. This strewing of flowers symbolises the new and beautiful path ahead for the Bride and her Groom. Brides can choose to have more than one flower girl if they wish.

Ring Bearer

A ring bearer is traditionally a male child attendant, between the ages of 6 and 10 years of age. His role is to precede the bride, (and flower girl), carrying a 'symbolic' ring (or rings) on a satin cushion. The ring(s) can be the 'real-thing' but it's advised to leave that responsibility to the Best Man... just in case!

Pages and Train Bearers

Most commonly seen at very traditional weddings, Pages are male child attendants, usually between the ages of 6 and 10 years of age. Their principal role is to carry the Bride's train as she walks down the aisle.

Train Bearers can be male or female child attendants, in the same age group. Pages and Train Bearers can be younger, but it's important to remember that carrying a train, without either tripping or becoming entangled in it, may not be that easy for anyone younger than 6! It's often a good idea to have 2 children holding the train.

Choosing Your Attendants

Depending on the size, style and theme of your wedding, the number of attendants can range from just one person, up to any number of preferred attendants – there really are no rules on this one. But of course, no matter how few or how many people you decide upon, choosing your attendants may feel a bit daunting in terms of the potential upset to friends and relatives in your selection process. It can be difficult to maintain a balance between family/friend loyalties and what you want for your wedding day.

First and foremost, be sure to keep in mind that this is yours and your Groom's big day and not a vehicle for your friends and relations to realise their own wedding fantasies and/or use it as a gauge as to how important they are to you. So, before you start, it's better to accept that there's a good chance that you might well disappoint someone. If you start from this position, anything less will be a bonus!

Making Your Choice

Look over the responsibilities for each of the attendant roles that you want to fill and start to work with what's feasible for each of your possible choices, in terms of distance, personality and responsibility.

It's no good picking your much-loved cousin Michelle to be your most trusted attendant, if her usual style is to live by the seat-of-her-pants, leaving everything until the last minute and who is likely to spend the day of the wedding surgically attached to the bar!

The same will apply to your Groom's Best Man – although, of course, you must allow him to make his own choice.

Pick an adult that you can rely on for your Maid of Honour/Matron of Honour or Chief Bridesmaid. You'll need this person to be level headed, honest, organised and practical – as well as someone who will stay calm and be able to extend reassurance and support if you're having a 'wobbly' moment. A maternal instinct will also be valuable if you're having child attendants.

If not picking a certain relative to be the Maid of Honour/Matron of Honour or Chief Bridesmaid will create the equivalent of a 'cold-war' within your family, then the urge to give in may just be too much. If that's the case then you may want to dispense of the title altogether and announce that you are just having bridesmaids and employing all their help – that way you can discreetly approach your preferred choice and ask her for some more specialised help and support.

If you have a lot of friends, but can't afford for them all to be bridesmaids, then pick one and opt for her as your Chief Bridesmaid. Your other option is to get all of your favourite girlfriends together for a night out and tell them that you'd love them to be bridesmaids, but can't afford it – if they'd really like the honour, some of them may offer to pay for their own outfits.

Don't forget to cost in gifts for your attendants into your budget – it's also important to remember to thank them for their hard work and support during the speeches.

Tips for Choosing Child Attendants

Choose children that you know – it might seem like a lovely gesture to pick your second cousin's oh-so-cute 4 year old daughter, but not so cute if she's having the screaming 'abdabs' during the ceremony, because she's suddenly decided she wants to run up and down the aisle.

Include children in any rehearsals that take place. Keep parents close, but get the children used to knowing where they need to be on the day. With smaller children, it's a good idea to allow them to sit with their parents during the ceremony.

Young children can get overwhelmed easily and very quickly, so be aware of not loading them with too much responsibility. The guidelines regarding attendant ages are only a guide and the maturity and general disposition of the child should be taken into account.

If any of your child attendants get stage fright and want to back out, you MUST let them, no matter how late in the day. Guilt trips and coercion are unfair and unnecessary – and you'll only end up with a very upset child on the day. Make sure that you have a 'plan-B', just in case.

Give your child attendants a really special reward and let them know how important they have been to your wedding. If a child has backed out, still reward them for being willing to participate.

Wedding Traditions

Ceremonial Positions
During the ceremony, the bride traditionally stands on the left side of the groom – this originates from the groom needing to leave their sword arm free, to fight off any potential suitors who may wish to vie for the affections of the bride. Oh, if only…

Confetti
Before the paper confetti we have today, guests used to throw rice over the bride and groom. This was believed to encourage fertility.

Flower Bouquets
Dating back to ancient times, the carrying of pungent herbs and spices was believed to ward off bad luck, evil spirits and illness. Later, in Victorian times, flowers were sent to lovers as messages - each type signifying a different message or meaning. These links were eventually adopted and adapted into the tradition of brides carrying bouquets.

Throwing the bouquet originated in America with the bride turning her back to the gathered female guests and throwing her bouquet in the air. Whoever catches the bouquet is said to be the next to marry. One word of caution, if you have lots of single women at your wedding be prepared for a scramble!

Present Giving

Before the age of giving toasters, other household goods and wedding lists guests traditionally brought fruit as gifts to the happy couple as this was believed to encourage fertility.

Something Old, Something New...

"Something old, something new, something borrowed, something blue and a silver sixpence in her shoe"

Dating back to Victorian times following this poem is believed to bring good luck to the bride and groom.

Something old... represents the connection to the bride's prior life and her family. Many brides opt to wear something old which has links to her side of the family.

Something new... represents the bride's successful new life ahead with her husband and good fortune. Often the wedding dress is considered as the 'something new'.

Something borrowed... represents the bride's personal support system and is a reminder to her that friends and family will be there for her in times of need. This item can be jewellery, a hair accessory or anything else the bride can wear on her person during the day.

Something blue... represents loyalty and fidelity to her husband dating back to biblical times, blue was the colour of purity. Garters are often detailed with blue ribbon – or it can be any other blue item which the bride can wear.

A silver sixpence in her shoe... represents the wish for happiness and wealth to the bride and her husband.

Threshold Carrying

The tradition of carrying the bride over the threshold was believed to protect the new and innocent bride from evil spirits, which may be creeping around the new home.

Wedding Cake

Back in Roman times, the wedding cake was termed as the 'bride's cake' and was ceremonially broken over her head, (charming!). This was to signify the groom's dominance over his new bride.

Obviously, this tradition is a little outdated and today the bride and groom cut the cake together to symbolise their intention to share everything in their future together. Far more acceptable for brides-to-be!

Traditionally the top tier of the cake, (or the fruit cake layer) is kept and saved for the first anniversary.

Wedding Dress

Traditionally, it's believed that the groom should not see the dress before the wedding day otherwise this will bring bad luck. To bring more good luck, he should even refrain from looking at her dress as she walks down the aisle towards him. It is believed that the bride should discard every pin, when removing her dress and veil, or she will be unlucky.

Wedding Favours

The tradition of wedding favours has been around for hundreds of years having now evolved into each guest receiving a reminder of the day, usually in the form of chocolate or five sugared-almonds representing health, wealth, fertility, happiness and long-life.

Wedding Etiquette

Attendants

Don't forget to cost in gifts for your attendants into your budget – it's also important to remember to thank them for their hard work and support during the speeches.

Receiving Line

The receiving line is carried out at the reception venue, and is done either on arrival or before the guests sit down to eat. The traditional order of receiving is as follows:-

Bride's parents
Groom's parents
Bride and Groom
Chief bridesmaid and Best Man

However, although this is the traditional line-up, some couple opt to receive the guests by themselves

Relatives

The Bride's Parents

The bride's mother is the last person to be seated before the ceremony begins. The bride's father escorts his daughter down the aisle. Both stand in the receiving line at the reception, with the bride's mother standing first in line.

Old Tradition had it that the father of the bride paid for the wedding and reception however now the cost is usually shared with the groom's parents and bride and groom.

Traditionally the father of the bride dances with her, after her first dance with her new husband.

The Groom's Parents

Traditionally, the groom's parents host the rehearsal dinner. Both are seated just before the bride's mother at the ceremony and stand in the receiving line at the reception.

Speeches

Beginning after the meal, speeches are either loved or loathed by those that have to do them! Traditional order is as follows:-

The bride's father:
Thanking the guests for coming, welcoming his new son-in-law into the family and reminiscing about the bride with fond/funny stories. The speech ends with a toast to the bride and groom.

The groom:
Thanking the bride's father for his speech and the bride's mother for her daughter – and to both for welcoming him into her family. Thanks and gifts are extended to the best man, bridesmaids, ushers and any other attendants or those who have helped with the organisation of the wedding. The groom thanks the guests for their presence and kind gifts and ends by proposing a toast to the bridesmaids.

The bride:
Although not strict tradition, the bride may also stand and speak after her husband. Thanking her parents for her love and support, the groom's family for welcoming her into their family and all that have helped her on the run up to the wedding day.

The best man:
Replying on behalf of the bridesmaids and telling humorous stories about the groom - fondly of course! The best man will read out cards and telegrams from guests who were unable to attend, make a toast to the bride and groom and announce the ceremonial cutting of the cake.

Top Table

Traditionally, the top table is a long table, facing all of the guests. The order usually runs from the left, (facing the table), as follows:-

Chief Bridesmaid	Groom's father	Bride's mother
Groom	Bride	Bride's father
Groom's mother	Best man	

However, some couples choose to keep their respective parents together.

Wedding Breakfast

Wedding breakfast etiquette states that the male guests should keep their jackets on until the groom removes his own jacket. After the wedding breakfast, it's traditional for the bride and groom to toast their guests as a thank you to all the guests for their love and support in attending the celebration of your marriage. But you don't have to come up with a lengthy rehearsed speech – try reading out a poem together. It can be serious or humorous - as long as it gets your message across.

Wedding Cake

A 'mock' cutting of the cake takes place with the photographer, purely for the official wedding photographs. The actual cutting of the cake takes place after the main course of the wedding breakfast. Reserve some wedding cake for guests who can't attend on the day that way they'll be touched that you were thinking of them even in their absence.

Weddings on a Budget

Weddings on a Budget

If you've gravitated to this section, then the chances are that you're already planning to be a budget-savvy bride!

There's a risk of getting lost in the 'must-have-it-all' mentality, with spiralling costs and unnecessary financial stresses. And for the majority of newly engaged brides-to-be, it's no surprise when there's an acute awareness of all the fantastical and highly publicised celebrity weddings taking place in castles, luxury hotels and other ultra-exotic and expensive locations... for instance love it or hate it, who can forget Katie Price's Cinderella-esque affair?

But the reality is that you don't have to pay over the odds for your wedding... flowers, wedding favours, gifts, venues, beautiful dresses and accessories – they're all costs that can be mitigated by creative thinking and canny shopping know-how.

It's not about how much you spend, but more about how much attention you pay to personalising your wedding, bestowing it with your own special touches and tweaks – making your wedding fabulously unique to you and your husband-to-be.

Accessories

Internet
The internet is a literal treasure-trove of affordable suppliers of gorgeous jewellery and hair accessories for you and your bridesmaids. Try bidding on eBay auctions if you're hunting for a really good deal.

Something Borrowed…

Save a little on jewellery, by borrowing a few matching pieces from a good friend as your 'something borrowed' addition to your wedding outfit.

Budget

First and foremost, it's essential that you and your fiancé agree on a budget and stick to it. In reality, you can get married for less than £500, there would be no, (or very few), frills of course, but it's certainly do-able.

Once you've decided your budget, do a tally at the end of each month and watch that you're not going into the 'red'. If you've budgeted £1,000 for your dress and it costs £1,250 – then you'll need to mitigate your overspend by pulling back on other items.

The perfect position would be to aim for starting married life without the strain of debt. To keep control of your budget, it's a good idea to keep a running record, monitoring your wedding costs.

Whatever your budget, take careful consideration when deciding what to spend your money on… if your honeymoon is the most important thing to you and you're working within a budget, then rollback what you're willing to pay for flowers, or your cake, or your reception venue… it's really up to you. A £750 cake may look fabulous, but for how long? A few hours, if that!

The most important thing is for your wedding to represent what YOU and your fiancé want and not what's expected of you. You don't want to look back and have any regrets – you're only doing this once, so cherish the memories.

Item	Budget	Actual (+/-)
Wedding Dress		
Bridal Accessories		
Ceremony Venue		
Morning Suits and Accessories		
First Night Hotel Room		
Reception Venue		
Cake		
Flowers		
Photography		
Videographer		
Caterer		
Wedding Rings		
Invitations		
Music and Entertainment		
Wedding Car (s)		
Attendants Gifts		
Wedding Favours		
Registrar Fees		
Clergy Fees		
Honeymoon		
Miscellaneous		
Total		

Cakes

Connections!

Search through your friends and family for someone who has a flair for baking cakes! If they can bake you a basic cake in your theme colour, then you have creative licence to decorate and customise it as you wish.

Downsize

If you've found the perfect design for a cake, but having it made for 120+ guests is going to have some unsavoury ramifications on your budget, ask your cake-maker to downsize the size of the cake and to supply a 'kitchen cake'. This comes as a standard sheet cake, with the same coloured icing – your guests will never know the difference!

Shop-Brought

Save yourself a small fortune and opt to buy your cake from a shop or supermarket. There are a range of high street retailers who make gorgeous cakes such as Tesco, Marks and Spencer, Sainsbury's and Asda.

Catering

Alcohol

One great money-saver can be to buy your own alcohol and pay corkage at the venue. If you order cases of alcohol from an online source, your purchases can be delivered direct to your venue. If you feel this is a smart option for you, make sure that you check the corkage charges at your choice of venue first.

Buffets

Who says that you have to stay with tradition and have a 3-course hot meal? Why not keep your costs down and offer a range of buffet foods instead?

If it's a hot day, your guests will welcome not having to sit and sweat through eating a hot meal – and if the weather's not so good, they can still revel in the novelty of a greater range of choices!

Costs and Negotiation

Wedding caterers, either in-house or external, can sometimes err on the 'tight' side when it comes to quantity, so when you're negotiating your food and drinks packages make sure that you go in with a good business head and negotiate hard. Also be aware of possible hidden costs, such as staffing, table decorations, flowers, etc.

Desserts

Be dessert-savvy and have your wedding cake as your dessert! Otherwise, there's a good chance that your meal-satisfied guests will take their wedding cake home and forget about it – so you'd be being doubly cost effective.

Extra Services

If you're using an external catering company, save yourself some money by not enlisting their waiter and waitress services. As long as your menu allows, your guests can serve themselves - either that or you can ask friends and family to help out.

Guest Limitations

If you're working to a set budget for your wedding breakfast, then you'll need to keep your guest numbers under control. Naturally, this may cause some tension between yourself and your fiancé, in terms of who gets to come.

The fairest way to tackle this issue is to divide your set numbers into thirds; one third being guests whom you both want to come; another third being your fiancés choices and the last third being your own choices. This way you'll both feel that neither one of you has monopolised the guest list.

In the event that parents are making a large contribution, you may want to split your list into quarters, to accommodate any guests that they would like to invite – however, on the understanding that you would have the power to veto anyone that neither you, nor your fiancé, like!

Unfortunately, having limitations on numbers is also likely to mean that you're going to have to disappoint friends or family, who may have already assumed that they would be there for the whole affair.

The best idea here is to contact those affected, before your invitations go out. This way you can apologetically explain your position and assure them that your decision isn't personal – and of course, you can inform them that they are invited to your evening reception.

Most people will understand your position – and anyone who doesn't was rightly not included in the first place. Guilt trips and emotional blackmail should be ignored at all costs!

Welcome Drinks
Make your own welcome drinks – homemade Pimms and punches, Cava and Bucks Fizz are firm favourites, but you can also create your own fabulous welcome drink ideas!

Wedding Favours
Tradition now seems to dictate that the wedding guests all receive favours - but instead of spending a lot on packaged, ready-made gifts why not make your own, or present a large basket of sweets in the centre of each table.

Deposits

Pay your supplier deposits early, so that you've room to pay for other necessary items before settling larger final accounts. It might not seem like a huge benefit, but add up all your deposit amounts and you'll soon see the benefit.

Dresses

Detailed Dresses
If you choose a detailed dress, with beading, crystals or lace you won't need as many accessories – so this will automatically save you money.

Go Bridesmaid!
There are some really stunning off-white bridesmaid's dresses to be found all of which will be at a snip of the price of a wedding dress. Who would know? And you could always customise it, if necessary.

High Street
High street shops such as BHS, Debenhams, Coast and Monsoon, have selections of beautiful bridal and bridesmaids gowns at very reasonable prices. Littlewoods catalogues also have a great range of evening wear.

Investigate!
Check out wedding fayres, designer days and seasonal and sample sale days. You'll find regular listings in wedding magazines and on the internet. A selection of listings detailing internet sites and magazines can be found at the back of our "The Perfect Day' section.

Rental

If the cost of a wedding dress is a step too far for your budget, then look into the costs for renting a gown. This way you can pick the designer dress of your dreams, without having to foot a designer bill.

Weight-Issues

If you're trying to lose weight, don't yo-yo diet in the run-up to your wedding. You'll either end up with higher costs because you need extra dress fittings and alterations or, you'll have a dress that's either too big or too small for you on the day. You don't need the stress!

Entertainment

Bands

If you'd love live entertainment but can't afford the fees, try contacting your local music colleges for student bands – they'll be far cheaper and may appreciate the break.

Use Your Own!

Instead of forking out money for a DJ, use pre-recorded music or your own iPod playlists!

Flowers

Artificial Flowers

Professionally bought fresh flowers can be expensive and sadly, they only really last in their full beauty for a day or two. So why not have a lifelong keepsake of your big day and flowers that will cost you less? Try the internet and local directories for suppliers.

Buy Wholesale

For another cost-saving idea, buy your wedding flowers from a wholesaler and with the help of some close friends, create your own simple, but elegant, displays and bouquets.

For instance, rose or tulip stems arranged simply in a glass vase or a posy tied with some raffia palm.

Choose Seasonal

Whether you're employing the services of a florist, or enlisting the help of family and friends, it'll be cheaper if you opt for flowers that are in season. Any florists will be able to tell you what's in and what's out of season.

Go Minimalist

Instead of being drawn into the tradition of having a full bouquet, go minimalist and choose a beautifully cut single rose, lily, gerbera or other long stemmed flower of choice. Or, opt for a small posy of freesias, bluebells or tulips.

How Does Your Garden Grow?

The cost of professionally arranged flowers can be a hefty weight on any wedding budget but you can achieve the most beautiful table arrangements, buttonholes and bouquets by picking flowers from your own garden - or from a willing friend's, family member's or even a generous neighbour's garden (or maybe all of the above!).

This will add vibrant colours, a variety of looks and textures and an array of wonderful fragrances to your day!

Of course, it's lovely to invite all and sundry to witness and celebrate your forthcoming nuptials, but one sure-fire factor that will drive up your wedding day costs is the number of guests you invite! Here are a few tips to help you keep your numbers under control:-

Draw up a provisional list, with an 'essentials' column and a 'possibly/maybe' column. That way you'll know what number of guests are definitely going to be invited, allowing you to work from that point.

Decide from the outset what number of invitations you will evenly allocate to your parents to give out – and stick to it. For instance if you have a maximum of 60 guests, allocate each set of parents 15 invites each and keep the remaining 30 as your own choices. Don't let any amount of emotional blackmail make you waver – you can't afford it!

Bear in mind that not all the guests you will invite will be able to make it - you can usually expect anything from 10% to 35% not to attend.

It might be controversial, depending on your family values, but consider either limiting the number of children, or making it a child-free wedding. Small bottoms on seats still equal an adult equivalent price per head!

Keep yourself in check on the run up to your wedding, when you find yourself drinking alcohol around people who are more like 'acquaintances', than friends, i.e. don't invite people in an over-friendly tipsy-moment!

Have a small guest list for the ceremony and wedding breakfast and then have a bigger guest list for your evening reception. That way you're being more inclusive without having to worry so much about food and drinks costs.

Don't be drawn into filling your venue to its maximum occupancy. Just because you can fit 120 people in the room, doesn't mean that you have to!

Don't feel obliged to invite people to your wedding just because they're promising you that they'll invite you to theirs in 18 months time! Invite the people who are most important to you, not those who would only be invited by default.

Don't bow to pressure from friends and relations who want you to invite more single men, or women. Your wedding day is about you and your new husband, not other people's love-lives!

Drop the 'plus guest' from your invitations – or at least limit them. You'll be surprised at how many guests would prefer to come alone!

If your budget is tight and you're struggling with the concept of keeping your numbers down ask yourself whether you would prefer lots of people, with the risk of poorer food quality, surroundings and ambience – or would you prefer to invite a smaller number of people, whom you could treat to a stylish and really special day? There's actually no right answer, (you might well prefer quantity over quality), but it'll give you a clearer sense of what you want for you and your guests.

Health and Beauty

Share Costs

Spread the cost of expensive, luxury make-up and skin care items by sharing them with your bridesmaids, sisters or mum – this will spread the cost and will mean that you can all afford to look and feel fantastic!

This won't be practical or hygienic for everything of course, but it'll go some way to help costs.

Home Crafts

Draw on your most helpful and creatively minded family and friends and try your hand at making some of your own table decorations and centrepieces.

Whether it be a home calligraphy kit for your place cards, drying rose petals for table confetti or making your own wedding favours – this is not only a good way to cut costs, but a lovely personal and unique touch for your wedding guests.

Honeymoon

Airmiles
If you've been savvy over the years, you may have had the forethought to save airmiles – if you have, this is a perfect time to cash them in!

Competitions
Look out for honeymoon holiday competitions in magazines, brochures, newspapers, etc. Lots of these competitions have low entry levels, due to date restrictions.

Someone has to win them, so, go for it!

Connections
Check out whether any of your friends or family own a holiday home that you could borrow for your honeymoon. Whether it be Mauritius, Majorca or Margate… it'll be just you and your new hubby, geography really won't matter once you're there!

Wedding List
Do away with a traditional wedding list and consider asking for a contribution to your honeymoon instead. Of course, you'll want to be sure to let your guests know that their presence alone is what you most require, but if they'd like to buy you a gift, then this would be a preferable option to you.

Of course, you may feel uncomfortable asking for 'hard cash', but there are some great short poems on the internet, which effectively soften asking for such a contribution – and if it's for something specific, your guests will have a greater sense of having been involved in doing something really special for you as a couple. If you're still uncomfortable with this money-saving idea, see it as an easier option for your guests – no trawling the shops for gift ideas or having to negotiate your chosen store's wedding list!

Invitations

Create Your Own
Rather than opt for expensive engraved invitations, be proactive and design your own invitations. It'll take an investment of time and creativity, but it'll save the cost of having them printed and your invitations will be unique.

Email
Cut out invitation costs altogether and email your guests with their invitations! You can create your own decorative attachment, including time and date details, venue, wedding list wishes, menus, order of service... everything you need. In an age where electronics seem to dominate as our chosen method of communication, you may also get quicker responses to your invitation too!

Hand Deliver
Save money on postage by hand delivering as many invitations as you can. You can also hand invitations to friends and family who may see some of your invited guests more regularly than you, or who live near them.

Photography

Cost Vs Quality
Probably one of the most important aspects of your day which will provide you with your only lasting visual reminders of this wonderful, whirlwind of a day. If there is an area of cost NOT to be scrimped on, this is it. However, if you can find a family member or close friend who are experienced enough to fill this role, then you'll be able to mitigate some costs – just be sure that you're comfortable with their level of competence.

Negotiate

You definitely want to find an experienced photographer, but be prepared to negotiate – not all will shift on their fees of course, but some will be flexible and/or offer reasonably priced packages and inclusive deals, all of which will be a welcome boost to your budget.

Portfolios

Make sure that you meet with at least 3 or 4 photographers and check out their portfolios. Look out for photographers who have good communication skills - remember that they'll be responsible for organising your potentially rowdy wedding-rabble into large groups! Check that they display good group shots as well as more focused, action and expressive shots and portraits.

Video

If you can't afford a videographer on top of all your other costs, you could ask someone you know and trust, to video your wedding for you. Most camcorders are user-friendly, so although it's unlikely they'll be up for an Oscar, whoever accepts this role will be capturing some really precious moments that wouldn't otherwise translate in a photograph. You could always ask a few people to take it in turns, to share out the role.

Purchasing

Bargain Basement!

Don't be put off by bargain-basement outlets – items such as tea lights, candles, table confetti, etc are pretty much the same wherever you buy them from. Your tea lights might not be scented at a bargain price, but they'll look just as pretty.

Be Patient

Don't buy on impulse because it's almost what you're looking for...you don't want to buy something that you might end up wasting.

Charity Shops

Don't rule out charity shops to find everything from dresses, shoes, knick-knacks, decorations and jewellery. You'll be sure to get a fabulous bargain, whatever you buy.

EBay

Whether your budget is strictly restricted, or you just want to find as many good deals as you can EBay can provide some excellent purchasing opportunities. Many wedding items have been used only once, if at all and can be bought at the snip of the bought-new price. Just be sure to check out your seller's individual 'star' rating and read other buyer's comments before you commit to a sale.

Seasonal Sales

Be shopping-smart and wait for end of season sales for a whole range of your wedding purchases from jewellery, make-up, beauty products and wedding attire to decorations, tea lights, fabric, favours and candles.

Store Reward Cards

This is the perfect time to save your points from all your store reward cards and use them when you'll need the money the most. You can purchase an array of things from cosmetics and clothing, to food and wine. Well worth patiently accruing your points!

Time Scales

The longer you have to plan your wedding, the more time you have to shop around comparing prices, bouncing around ideas and making sure that you get the most competitive deals. Make sure that you hit the high street, wedding fayres, magazines, brochures, the internet and any other resources you can find. It also gives you more time to save up.

Resources

Friends and Family

Friends and family are a great resource to draw on when it comes to planning your wedding – for starters, you know that they genuinely care and somewhere amongst them, there'll be one, two, three… or even more… who possess special talents or skills, which will prove invaluable assets to keeping your wedding costs under control. So whether it be someone that can sew sequins or crystals to customise your dress, someone that can design and make decorations, someone trained in floristry, someone that is a great organiser or even someone who has useful connections – make sure that you check out all the possibilities.

Booking Timings

If your dream venue is not up for negotiation and you MUST have it – how about changing your date? Or the season within which you marry? Weddings held on weekdays or off-peak season generally come at a generous discount – and sometimes with extras thrown in. You'll also find that a lot of suppliers are cheaper too. For off-peak bookings, try booking from October to March/April time. If you're stuck on having a summer wedding, don't worry too much about having a weekday wedding. As long as you give your guests plenty of notice, they can book the time off work.

Local Venues

Village halls and local pub function rooms can be transformed into magical, dream-like venues with the right ideas, inspiration and decoration – and they keep costs low. Or, why not book your favourite restaurant for your reception venue? That way you'll know that the food and drink is good and they'll be the only costs that you incur.

Marquees

If your dream is to have a marquee, be sure to cost out everything down to the last detail.

Religious Ceremonies

If you're having a religious ceremony, why not consider having your wedding day near a holiday or festive season such as Christmas or Harvest Festival – that way your venue will already have lots of decorations and flowers inside, which will not only look beautiful but it'll also save you money.

Venue Conditions

When booking your venue, check that your choice doesn't tie you into using their suppliers, e.g. florists, caterers, decorations, etc. Your budget is reliant on you maintaining control of each cost, so make sure that you don't trip up with expensive in-house suppliers.

Wedding Rings

Wedding rings really don't have to break the bank. Compare prices online, or set a budget with your fiancé and stick to it.

Wedding day tips

Essential Wedding Day Tips...

Ceremony Music
Your guests are likely to be waiting for around 20-30 minutes for the service to begin, so rather than them have to wait in silence, carefully choose some ambient prelude music that will suit the tone and mood of your ceremony.

You'll also need to remember to check with your ceremony venue, (whether religious or civil), as each venue will have its own rules around what type of music can be played before, during and whilst exiting your ceremony.

Children's Corner
If you have a marquee or large enough venue, set aside a corner of the room with large bean bags, for children to sit, hang out... or have a bit of a nap! Have a 'Pick n Mix' area of sweets for children - place a bag on each place setting where there are children and allow them to help themselves. A reasonably priced treat that kids will love!

Disposable Cameras
Disposable cameras are often an addition you will see on wedding tables, which in principal is a nice idea, but in reality how many pictures will be of the floor/wall/table? Or blank? Or self-portraits with full-on close ups of nostrils? Or pictures of random items in the room, taken by your helpful 6 year old nephew?

Added to that are often grainy, poorly lit photos, which will most probably make it nowhere near your wedding day photo album. Instead, ask your guests to take digital photos with cameras, or their mobile phones and send them to you electronically – you'll get far better quality pictures.

Drinking Tip
Don't get carried away and drink too much early in your wedding day – the day will literally just fly-by anyway, so you want to remember as much as possible, as clearly as possible!

First Dance

If you're feeling adventurous, why not surprise your guests with your first dance and take professional dancing lessons? This can be as simple as learning the waltz – or as elaborate as learning a full on dance routine with your hubby! It'll give you and your intended, something extra special to share before, during and after your wedding day – and the looks on your guests' faces will be priceless.

Guest's 'Promise Book'

Have some fun and create a 'promise book' – written by your guests! Leave slips of paper on each table and ask your guests to write down at least one thing that you should do for one another as a couple. Depending on your guests, the results should be romantic, fun and possibly a bit saucy!

Keep Perspective

Keep a firm hold of what your day is really about and try not to lose perspective in the organisation and planning. Beautiful aesthetics and good food are always a lovely addition to any wedding but how many weddings have you been to, where the most memorable thing about the day was the meal? It's more likely that you can't even remember what you had! Your guests are there to see you get married, not closely inspect your choice of decoration and colour scheme. You're entering into a marriage with the person you love and adore and that's all you'll care about on the day.

Last Night

The night before the wedding, get together with close friends, family and loved ones – go for dinner, have a few drinks, talk about everything and anything – laugh, cry, dance-around, relax – wherever the mood takes you. This is the beginning of your wedding celebrations, so make your last unmarried night a magical and memorable one.

Let Go!

Don't anchor your hopes and dreams for your wedding day on absolute precision and perfection - nothing ever works like that. Once the wheels are in motion, there'll likely be a few hiccups, how you react to those hiccups will either make or break your day. You'll have plenty of people around you to help iron out any issues, so try not to lose your cool.

Outdoors Fun!

If there's a grassy area outside of your reception, see if you can set up a game like croquet or soft tennis – or other over-sized games. This is great fun for children and adults alike! You'll need permission from the venue first, of course.

Peace & Quiet

If you can, have a quiet area, away from your entertainment where people can talk and have a break from the general hubbub and noise. Decorate a table and leave out some mints or sweets. You can even put up a little sign designating the area.

Seating

Try having a U-shape or E-shape table configuration for your wedding breakfast - this will mean that you and your guests can all see one another, which facilitates conversation and mingling.

Shop Early

If you're a stickler for detail and you want everything to be 'just-so' in terms of theme and/or colour coordination, then make sure you shop for the finer detail early on. You don't want to find yourself stressing a week before the wedding, because you can't find the exact shade of lilac ribbon for your flower girl's pony tail!

Table Plan

Don't get sucked into obsessing about your table plan. Trying to keep everyone happy, especially if there are family 'issues', can be an anxiety-inducing experience - but you'll never make everyone 100% happy. And you'll be surprised at how willing people are to put their differences aside for your sakes – after all, it is only for a few hours.

Weather Watch!

Try not to worry too much about the weather. If you're a resident of the UK, you should be used to the erratic summers by now, (not to mention the ever-changing weather forecasts). In the week running up to your wedding, the temptation may be to obsess over every meteorological nuance, which will either give you the serious grumps, or at best, a shaky sense of well being.

Unfortunately, you're on to a loser in terms of being able to feel reassured that the sun will make a glorious appearance on the day. Instead, choose to have a pragmatic stance about the weather and talk with your photographer about alternatives for inside photos, if need be.

And even if the heavens do decide to open, you'll be far too ecstatic to care!

Wedding Cocktail

Make-up your own cocktail, (or use your favourite cocktail) and name it after your you and your husband! If you can stretch to it, have it in a punch bowl and allow the guests to help themselves.

Just Married!

The Honeymoon....

As newlyweds, this is going to be one of the most special holidays of your lives. It's a time for letting your exciting new martial status sink in, for enjoying each other's company exclusively, recuperating and resting after all the stress of planning your wedding and having some much deserved pampering and luxury. Traditionally, the groom organises and pays for the honeymoon, sometimes even keeping the destination a secret, (brave man!). However, as with most wedding traditions, it is often now the norm for couples to organise their honeymoon together. And far from being yet another part of your wedding planning, this part is a real pleasure – with no friends·and family to upset or consider and a romantic break for you and your new hubby. Sounds blissful! But, before you jet off to your personal paradise, you've got to find your destination and book it! So where do you start?

Ask Yourself

Before delving headfirst into brochures and travel websites, ask yourselves a few key questions:-

Who will do the organising?
How long will you honeymoon for?
What's your budget? Not forgetting spending money.
If you already have children, will they come too or will they need to stay with close relatives?
Do you want sunshine or snow?
Where can you see yourself going together? e.g. island paradise, city chic, package holiday, cold but cosy, country cottage, etc.
What sort of holiday do you want? e.g. beach lounging, luxury, action packed, walking, extreme sports, touristy, etc.
Does the area of the world you'd like to go to need vaccinations and/or a visa? If so, do you have enough time to plan it?

Booking

Once you've booked your wedding venue(s), it's a good idea to start looking for your honeymoon. If you're booking at peak season or during a major holiday period, you're certainly better off having your honeymoon booked and under your belt as soon as you can.

Destination and Weather

If you live in the UK then you'll be used to summer weather during the months of June, July and August – the same can be said for the Mediterranean climate. However, you need to remember that some other countries have 'summer' weather at completely different times. In fact some popular destinations have distinctly unpleasant weather during our British summertime! For instance, July to October in Thailand is their 'rainy season' and July in South Africa is their equivalent of winter. So make sure that you check out your destination's climate before you book.

Honeymoon Packages

When you book your destination, mention that you'll be on your honeymoon. Some travel companies and hotels offer discounted honeymoon packages and upgrades.

Last Minute Bookings

It might be okay to pick up a last minute deal at times when you and your fiancé are happy to embrace a 'seat-of-your-pants' experience, but 'the unexpected' on your honeymoon is not recommended.

Cheap deals can be great, but sometimes you get exactly what you pay for, which could kill your honeymoon enjoyment dead. Don't underestimate exactly how exhausted you're both going to be – so it'll be important to have a relaxing comfortable place for you both to recuperate.

Mutual Agreement

So, you'd like to drink margaritas by the pool and he'd prefer to climb a few mountains and admire the view together or vice versa! It's important that neither one of you agrees to a honeymoon destination/style which you'll end up hating.

Of course you love each other and want to make each other happy, but this holiday is about the both of you and as it represents the beginning of your marriage, compromising with something that you'll both enjoy is vital.

Start married life as you mean to go on!

Honeymoon Packing Checklist

Passports
Tickets & travel itinerary
Insurance documents
Toiletries
Medicines
Sun protection products
Cosmetics
Electricals, e.g. hair-dryers, tongues, shaver, etc
Camera & camcorder
Mobile phones & chargers
Beachwear, sportswear, etc
Casual clothes
Evening wear
Appropriate footwear, day & evening
Accessories

Spending Money

A fabulous destination is great, but you also need to make sure that you've enough spending money to enjoy it to the max. Check out how expensive your destination is in terms of food, drinks and leisure activities before you book – and save, save, save!

Travel Insurance

It might seem like yet another cost to accommodate, but travel insurance is vital. Hopefully nothing adverse will occur on your honeymoon, but it's far better to be prepared. If you're choosing to marry abroad, you'll need to take out a policy which will also cover gifts and your wedding attire.

Just Married!

L.A.W – Life After Wedding!

It's been a long time coming and now you're there…you're married! So, now what? Even if you've been married before, you've never been married to THIS person – it's a brand spanking-new experience for both of you. It'll feel exciting, joyful, wonderfully emotional and at times, downright scary – but with your hearts full of love and respect, you're off to a great start. Each new day will bring new experiences, new feelings, new discoveries and a few unexpected surprises - both good and bad. Whilst you go through the sometimes daunting process of adjusting to living your lives as a unit, it's important to begin your life together by agreeing an undertaking of understanding and patience with one another.

Compromising Too Much

Naturally, you will want to live in harmony with each other, so compromises will have to be made – but if there is a particular issue which either you or your husband feel under undue pressure to acquiesce to, think carefully before committing to final decisions. If you've got your own way, any satisfaction may well be short-lived, as you soon realise that your loved-one is unhappy. And if you're the one who has yielded, you're likely to start feeling resentful. In the long run, if something is important to you it's better to hold your ground and respect your partner for doing the same. You'll save yourselves a lot of heartache by doing so.

Physical Costs

After such a long period of running yourselves ragged on caffeine and adrenalin on the run up to your wedding, it's not uncommon for your bodies to suddenly start coming down with all manner of viruses and illnesses, once you've finally started to relax. So, prepare yourself with immune boosting vitamins, water, plenty of sleep and a good balanced diet. It'll give your bodies the best fighting chance they have.

Post-Wedding Blues

The honeymoon is over and it's time to get on with the rest of your lives. Your tan is fading, your dress is stored in the loft, you feel flat and de-motivated - but worst of all your new hubby seems to suddenly have gone from your favourite person in the world, to someone whose daily habits make you want to throw things… preferably at him. Surprised? Don't be. It's fairly common for some newly weds to discover that the post-wedding period feels like one big anti-climax.

The good news is that it won't last, you're just experiencing the 'come-down' after months, and maybe even years, of planning this one big event. Talk it through with each other and find ways in which to have some fun together. That way you'll soon reengage with all the reasons why you fell in love in the first place.

Post-Wedding Angst

Whether you've lived together before your wedding or not, chances are that the first year of marriage will be the most challenging. You've made a very public declaration of love and commitment to one another and one that's legally binding too - so that's bound to have an affect on how you view your 'new' life and each other.

It's natural to expect that after the initial 'honeymoon period', reality will kick in and you'll start to have differences in opinion, often about seemingly trivial things. Rather than avoid issues that bother you, it's best to air them and negotiate solutions where possible. If you allow things to simmer under the surface, chances are that they'll come out in a flash of anger and in the wrong way. Remember, that you're paving the way for a life-long future together, so healthy, clear communication is key.

Pre-Wedding Talks!

Unfortunately, the transition into married life doesn't come with a set of step-by-step instructions to help you on your way, (not that your hubby would read them anyway!) so to help minimise the amount of disagreements and adjustment difficulties, it's a good idea to have pre-wedding conversations about practical and emotional issues, such as:-

Where do you intend to live?
How will you work your monthly finances?
Will you have single or joint accounts?
How will you continue with your respective careers?
How will you fairly allocate the housework, cooking, etc?
How much leisure-time do you both envisage having?
How much 'together' time do you both want to have?
Where do you stand on having children?
How will you juggle friends and family, alongside your needs as a couple?
How will you make time to be intimate, when you're stressed, tired and stretched for time?
How do you intend to communicate any issues you may have with one another?
What rules will you have around arguing? (Dos & Don'ts)
How and where will you spend birthdays and Christmases?